Endorsements

"The Rev. Dr. Cynthia L. Hale and Rev. Darryl D. Sims have pulled together some of the nation's greatest preachers in this much awaited edition. These sermons adeptly address issues that are germane to both men and women. As you read these powerful and poignant messages, you will be gripped by their presentation of what Phillips Brooks called, 'authentic preaching-truth through personality.' "

BISHOP WALTER S. THOMAS
New Psalmist Baptist Church
BALTIMORE, MD

"This compilation of sermons preached by some of America's leading women pastors and preachers, provides individuals with a spiritual toolkit to negotiate difficult moments. Each sermon gives those who are married, single, head of households, or who serve as the primary source for family income, God's method for facing challenging times. I am particularly grateful for the book's intentionality to address both genders. This book is not exclusively for women. Men and women will equally receive instruction and inspiration from these sermons. I salute both the co-editors and the contributors for the vision and the content of this powerful book. God has already blessed it. May it bless the lives of all who read its pages."

REV. DR. JANETTE C. WILSON, ESQ.
CEO & EXECUTIVE PRODUCER,
International Sunday School Broadcast Inc.
CHICAGO, IL

"All of my life, I've heard good preaching that either provoked or encouraged me to experience the power of God. In the book, These Sisters Can Say It, I admit without any reservation these sisters proclaim the Word of God with boldness, skillfulness, and an anointing to be reckoned with by even the most discriminating listener. All I can do is stand up and holler...Preach!"

PASTOR BELINDA THOMAS

Be Restored Worship Center

LITHIA SPRINGS, GA

"Any doubts about the calling and anointing of women to preach the Gospel of Jesus Christ ought to be dispelled after reading, These Sisters Can Say It. The women preachers who contributed to this book and gave a thorough exegesis of the text and the masterful presentation of the Gospel, will rekindle the fire of the Holy Spirit in you to keep on preaching! This book is a must have for every preacher, and should be a part of your personal library."

PASTOR JOCELYN C. THORNTON,

Emmannuel Covenant Church,

ORLAND PARK, IL

"For those who are committed to the notion of recognizing the theological and homeletical voices of women, young and seasoned alike, I recommend this book. These sisters have written sermons that are compelling, transformative, and challenging. Their prophetic insights offer sound guidance to a chaotic culture and hope to hungry souls."

CO-PASTOR ELAINE MCCOLLINS FLAKE

The Greater Allen A.M.E Cathedral

JAMAICA, NY

To
Rev. Veda McCoy,
Always allow your light to
shine brightly before all the people.

Daryl D. Sims

THESE
Sisters
CAN <u>CAN</u> *Say*
IT!

**15 Powerful Sermons from Contemporary
African American Women Preachers**

EDITED BY DARRYL D. SIMS
WITH DR. CYNTHIA L. HALE

MMGI BOOKS · CHICAGO

These Sisters Can Say It!
15 Powerful Sermons from Contemporary
African American Women Preachers

Edited by Darryl D. Sims
with Dr. Cynthia L. Hale
Foreword by Dr. Renita J. Weems

Copyright © 2009
ISBN (13) 978-0-615-31781-6

Cover and Interior Design:
Selah Branding and Design LLC
www.selahbrandinganddesign.com

Editorial Assistance by Monica Sanders and
Eugenia M. Orr

Printed in the United States of America

Table of Contents

Dedication   vii
Acknowledgments   ix
Foreword by Renita J. Weems   xi

1. LESLIE D. CALLAHAN   1
"Breathe Again"

2. CLAUDETTE A. COPELAND   13
"Ask for the Hard Thing"

3. SHELETA FOMBY   25
"You Can Overcome It"

4. CECELIA E. GREENEBARR   39
"Organ Donor"

5. CYNTHIA L. HALE   49
"The Secret to Your Success"

6. MILLICENT HUNTER   67
"Baggage Handlers"

7. SHARMA D. LEWIS   85
"It is Only a Test"

8. SUSIE C. OWENS   95
"When You are In Over Your Head"

9. VANNETTA R. RATHER   107
"No Limit"

10. TRENACE N. RICHARDSON   119
"Tired of Being Sick and Tired"

11. SANDRA RILEY   133
"Say It Until You See It"

12. ELIZABETH SAPP JONES   143
"Change: A Necessity for your Breakthrough"

13. JASMINE W. SCULARK   161
"Unshackled from Rejection"

14. GINA M. STEWART   175
"A Window of Opportunity"

15. BARBARA WILLIAMS-SKINNER   189
"Go in the Strength that You Have"

FOOTNOTES   209
ABOUT THE CONTRIBUTORS   211
ABOUT REV. DR. CYNTHIA L. HALE   219
ABOUT REV. DARRYL D. SIMS   221
JOURNAL FOR MY JOURNEY   224

Dedication

This book is dedicated to sixteen ladies who fill my life with joy, excitement, and purpose.

These divinely placed women are: my mother Vivian Brown, my second mother Ruby Sims, my spiritual mother Virginia Maltbia, my favorite auntie Elizabeth "Tody" Bady, my three daughters Darnisha, Latecia, Riele, my two grand-daughters Ja'Niya and Jasmine (pray for me), my six sisters Jamise, Benita, Marie, Renee, Tarina, and Karen (Candy), and my best friend since High School, Darnisha Thompson.

In addition, *These Sisters Can Say It*, is dedicated to every woman who was forced to deny her call and her proper title as a preacher because of her God-given gender.

And finally, this book is dedicated to all of the "sisters" who have had to struggle in ministry and fight to be heard and recognized as a preacher of the Gospel of Jesus the Christ.

-Darryl D. Sims

Acknowledgments

I am so incredibly blessed to share in this phenomenal project with my little brother, Darryl Sims, who has masterminded the work and invited me to partner with him. Thanks, Darryl for your sensitivity and foresight. I would not be a part of such a project, if it weren't for the fact that God called me before He weaved me together in my mother's womb. My parents, Harrison and Janice Hale, raised me to be faithful to the Him.

When I consider all the other people I want to thank for this extraordinary opportunity to serve as a co-editor for a book of women preachers, allow me to mention three: Rev. Alvin Jackson, my Paul in the ministry, Rev. Alvord Beardslee, the chaplain at Hollins University where I answered my call to the ministry, and Rev. Bridget Puzon, the first woman I heard preach the Gospel with absolute power and who helped me believe God was truly calling me.

And to all the awesome women, sisters, friends who graciously consented to have their sermons printed in this book. I am eternally grateful for who you are, and all you do to establish the reign of God on earth in your own powerful and feminine way.

Rev. Dr. Cynthia L. Hale
Senior Pastor
Ray of Hope Christian Church
2778 Snapfinger Road
Decatur, GA   30034

Pastor Cynthia and I would like to acknowledge the Herculean efforts of Monica Sanders, LaTanya Orr and Eugenia Orr. These powerful women of God gave their all, while attempting to keep this project focused and moving in the divine direction of the Lord.

Monica provided a great deal of assistance with the editorial aspects of the project. LaTanya stood her "creative ground" and put me in my place on the design and color scheme for the front cover of this book. Both of these women displayed exemplary skills and professionalism throughout the development of this project.

Lastly, Cynthia and I would like to thank the contributors for being true to the craft of preaching and true to our request to pull from their divinely-nurtured, collective "prophetical bellies," sermons that speak to the most relevant and contemporary issues affecting both men and women.

Rev. Darryl D. Sims
Managing Partner
MMGI Books

Foreword
BY RENITA J. WEEMS, PH.D.

Years from now, historians will be tripping over themselves trying to explain the seismic shifts that took place in American Protestantism at the end of the 20th, and beginning of the 21st centuries. Three trends of the period, in particular, will have them scratching their heads, searching for an explanation: 1) the rise of radical Christian fundamentalism and its influence upon American politics; 2) the roles played by Neo-Pentecostalism and the Charismatic renewal movement in the decline of mainstream denominationalism; and 3) the groundswell of women entering the ministry during the period.

Sermon collections like the one you're holding in your hand, *These Sisters Can Say It,* will be proof that God was active during this period, raising up new and powerful voices to God's power and God's will during this important period in American history. The sermons in this collection show God at work healing, delivering, saving, transforming, and calling to repentance, this generation through those who, generations before, had been silenced and marginalized by tradition.

Things have changed a lot in the twenty-five years since my ordination into the ministry. Women are bishops in the Methodist, Episcopal, and Full Gospel traditions. Baptist churches are beginning to call women to their pulpits as pastors. Women occupy positions on denominational boards, as well as serve as executive and assistant ministers at many churches across the country. To be sure, we still have a long way to go to reach parity with our brothers in ministry. There's no denying, though, that the landscape has changed a lot for preaching women in the last couple of decades.

The things about which we preach give a testament to the things for which we care. In this collection, you will find that these women who preach care about all the things messengers of God are supposed to care about: Salvation, Faith, Hope, Empowerment, and Repentance. Where women preachers are different is, they see the world differently from men, and, therefore, come at the preaching task with the eyes, ears, and heart of women who have a lot to say about family, home, security, nature, love, peace, and hope.

On occasion, I have worried about how this generation of women clergy will be remembered. I wondered if history would record that we stood to speak and no one trembled or felt challenged as audiences did during the time of the prophet Amos. I wondered if we might miss our opportunity in history, if we would be remembered more for the fashionable clergy outfits we sported in the pulpit than for the prophetic stance we took when it was time to say "Thus says the Lord..."

Reading the sermons by these wonderful women preachers featured here, in *These Sisters Can Say It*, testifies that my worries were in vain. God is still waking preachers up in the middle of the night calling them to ministry. It's good to know that preachers are still rising in the middle of the night and saying "Here I am, send me." I Thank God! It's wonderful to see that women preachers, too, are not only answering the call, but also writing their words down, for all to run who read them.

"Breathe Again"

A Sermon by LESLIE D. CALLAHAN

John 11:33-44 (New Living Translation)

When Jesus saw her weeping and saw the other people wailing with her, a deep anger welled up within him, and he was deeply troubled. "Where have you put him?" he asked them. They told him, "Lord, come and see." Then Jesus wept. The people who were standing nearby said, "See how much He loved him!" But some said, "This man healed a blind man. Couldn't He have kept Lazarus from dying?" Jesus was still angry as He arrived at the tomb, a cave with a stone rolled across its entrance. "Roll the stone aside," Jesus told them. But Martha, the dead man's sister, protested, "Lord, he has been dead for four days. The smell will be terrible." Jesus responded, "Didn't I tell you that you would see God's glory if you believe?" So they rolled the stone aside. Then Jesus looked up to heaven and said,

1

"Father, thank You for hearing me. You always hear me, but I said it out loud for the sake of all these people standing here, so that they will believe You sent me." Then Jesus shouted, "Lazarus, come out!" And the dead man came out, his hands and feet bound in graveclothes, his face wrapped in a headcloth. Jesus told them, "Unwrap him and let him go!"

Travel back in time with me, to the early 1990's, and experience Toni Braxton's soulful single from her 1993 self-titled album. In the hit song, "Breathe Again," Braxton graphically described the breathless quality that sometimes accompanies deep love. When I say "breathless quality," I am not talking about the heart-pounding, temperature-raising BREATHLESSNESS that you may experience in the presence of your beloved. This is not the exhilarating loss of breath that comes from hyperventilation. It's not the thrilling breathlessness of breathing too hard, too fast or with too much gusto. This is not a situation in which the joyful thought of the beloved's presence takes the breath away. No, Braxton's song captures the gut wrenching, having the wind knocked out of you, quality of breathlessness that a lover experiences after breaking away from the beloved. It speaks of the shock, the turmoil, and the panic that accompanies this loss. It articulates the agony that comes with a sense of finality. The Lover says, "Not only am I not able to catch my breath now, but if this really is final," in Braxton's words: "I promise you that I shall never breathe again."

Individuals, as well as whole nations alike, know that feeling of breathlessness. Lamentations chapter 3 recalls some of the devastation endured by

God's people under Babylonian conquest. Reading through the eloquently poetic hardships, we are able to get a glimpse of how painful life can sometimes be. Reflecting on his personal predicament in the midst of national catastrophe, the prophet Jeremiah puts it starkly in verses 15 through 20: "He has filled me with bitterness; he has sated me with wormwood. He has made my teeth grind on gravel, and made me cower in ashes; my soul is bereft of peace; I have forgotten what happiness is; so I say, 'Gone is my glory, and all that I had hoped for from the Lord.'" With words that echo in Braxton's refrain "I can't stop thinking about you," Jeremiah continues, "The thought of my affliction and my homelessness is wormwood and gall! My soul continually thinks of it and is bowed down within me" (ESV).

Even friends and followers of Jesus, like the women in our text, are visited by grief, trauma, trials and tribulation. When we encountered Mary and Martha in Luke 10, they were vying for the proper balance in appropriately serving the Master, while He was a guest in their home in Bethany. Do you remember the story? Mary was cast as the worshipper, choosing "the better part" and sitting attentively at the feet of Jesus. Martha, on the otherhand, was the worker, exercising her gift of hospitality making certain that Jesus' needs were met, yet frustrated — complaining that her sister was derelict in her duty to help. In that earlier scene, the sisters were at odds and the tension was thick. Here again, we find them in an atmosphere filled with tension, but this time, these two familiar women, the worshipper and the worker, speak with the same voice, connected through grief and sorrow.

Their brother Lazarus had just died as a result of something that appears to have been unexpected and sudden. They sent word to Jesus when they discovered Lazarus had become ill, but Jesus lingered where he was and did not arrived in time to intervene before Lazarus met death. With Lazarus, their brother, dead and buried, Mary and Martha were undoubtedly left BREATHLESS. Breathless from the disappointment. Breathless from the grief. Breathless from the exhaustion of endlessly long days and wearily sleepless nights. Breathless! They had just experienced having the wind knocked out of them.

Mary and Martha teach us a very crucial lesson. If you haven't discovered it by now, allow me to inform you of an alarming and inescapable fact: Every human life has its storms. Although the walk of faith yields many fruits, it, as well as friendship and fellowship with Jesus, does not proclaim to keep us from experiencing the gales of life or the pain of loss. What our walk of faith and our fellowship with Jesus will teach us how to go through each experience with the right perspective, trusting in God.

Don't be fooled into thinking you will ever be able to avoid life and all that it encompasses. Mary, you cannot walk closely enough. Marth, you cannot work hard enough. You cannot join enough committees or volunteer in enough programs. Even when you build your hopes on eternal things while holding onto God's unchanging hand, you will still occasionally experience the hurts of human existence. How well will you still reflect God's goodness throughout it all?

You cannot write enough philanthropic checks or burn enough midnight oil. Nor can you work hard enough in the service of the Lord to inoculate yourself against the realities of those things that may cause pain and devastation. Even when you give the best of your service—running as hard and as faithfully as possible through the race of life, every now and then, you will run smack into an unyielding wall. I don't know whether you've ever run into a wall, but I remember a few of my own collisions and I can testify that running into a wall knocks the wind out of you.

Sometimes, it's your fault, but sometimes you may have done everything you could do to stave off disaster, but disaster still had its day. Sometimes, you really were a good wife or husband, and your spouse still left. Sometimes, you really were a good worker, and you still got laid off or fired. Sometimes, you really were a prayer warrior, and your loved one still died. Sometimes, you really did sit down at the family dinner table with your children and tell them to stay in school and stay away from drugs, but when they got up from the table they dropped out of school and became addicted to drugs. Sometimes, despite following all the rules, circumstances still do not work out as you may have hoped or imagined. Sometimes, life just knocks the wind right out of you.

Enter Jesus. Remember Jesus? He's the One who, had he shown up a little sooner, could have prevented the entire breath-taking circumstance from occurring. Here comes Jesus, the One on whom all of their, and our, hopes rest. Now, beloved, you have to know, that whenever Jesus enters the scene, no matter the nature of the scene - whether it represents the most mundane or the most horrific human circumstance - it's time to pay close attention. Whenever Jesus enters the picture, one has to expect that something wonderful will occur.

Martha hears that Jesus is coming, and meets him down the road. I could focus on their conversation, filled with words of accusation from Martha and later repeated by Mary, "If you had been here, our brother would not have died." Or, I could focus on the words of promise from the Savior, who knew that he would do for Lazarus just what he promises to do for us all: "Your brother will rise again." I could join Martha in her feeble attempt to sound like a faithful person: "I know my brother will rise in the resurrection." And there is always the temptation to go to the revelation of Christ's divine identity and mission that allows all of God's people to face death with hope: "I am the resurrection and the life. Those who believe in me, though they die will live again." Any part of that conversation could lead, and has led, to a million sermons of great quality.

But rather than discussing the conversation between Martha and the Lord, I would like us to examine Jesus' instruction that Martha and Mary take him to the tomb, "Show me where you laid him." By requesting that Mary and Martha lead him to the tomb, Jesus calls the sisters to the place of their greatest pain. He has them take him directly to the site of their most significant devastation. Jesus does not simply fix the trouble in their lives from a distance. This is no drive-by ministry on the way to something more pressing and important. By bringing Mary and

Martha back to the tomb, and by asking them to trust him even when that trust carries them to the valley of the shadow of death, Jesus actually affected the resuscitation of not only Lazarus' body, but of the drained faith of the worker and the worshipper as well.

I wonder if we can locate the tombs in our lives where we have laid our departed faith, our dead hopes, and our dormant loves. I wonder if we are willing to search out the lifeless, breathless places in our lives. I wonder if we can revisit the zones of our disappointment, those addresses where Jesus showed up after the disaster had already blown through. Then, once we find them, I wonder if we will have the courage to not only face them, but to bring Jesus to them. I think that if we look more closely at Jesus and his response when he arrived at the tomb, perhaps we may be able to come to the place where we will trust him with the most painful aspects of our own lives.

Upon their arrival at the tomb, we are told that Jesus weeps. More than just the shortest verse in the biblical record, useful for quick recitation, John 11:35 instructs essential theological truth that will bless us if we take it seriously. "Jesus wept" teaches us that we serve and worship a caring Lord, who tends to our deepest grief, and is longing for us to trust him. This passage demonstrates to us that we serve a Lord who, bore our grief and carried our lost hope upon his shoulders. Jesus' tears make it clear that we serve a high priest who can, and is, touched by the feeling of our infirmities. Jesus' weeping makes it clear to us that we serve a human Lord, whose heart and eyes and glands shared in the essence of human emotion.

How fortunate are we that the text doesn't just end with "Jesus wept?" At the tomb, we also see Jesus praying. What I like about Jesus is, even though he already knows what he is going to do and what God is able to do, he assumes the role of teacher and clarifies the revelation that we need to grab a hold of in order to take possession of victory. By following his lead, we always know the procedure and the process for experiencing salvation, deliverance, and healing. So, Jesus prays. Through his tears, he calls out to God. At that moment, Jesus says what we should absolutely know in every moment when we talk to Almighty God: "I know you hear me."

Then, finally, with power rooted in his God-given authority over death and the grave (the same authority given to us in John 14:12-13), Jesus does for Lazarus and his sisters what Jesus does best. He restores vitality within a dead situation by raising Lazarus from the grip of the grave. He wakes up the dormant possibility and restores the lifeless back to life.

Now you need to know that even after Lazarus is raised in the eleventh chapter of John, Jesus is clear that his work has only just begun. As long as death holds any power to claim humankind and create, in finality, a lifeless, hopeless, breathless state for human beings, Jesus' work is not yet done. Since Adam, death and the devil had been taking the best of human lives and rendering them, eventually and irrevocably, breathless. No matter how good or how faithful, how holy or how spiritual a person could be, the devil could just bide his time, knowing that, eventually, death would get its grips on them. So, God being God, knows that this great miracle of revival in Lazarus, Mary and Martha will ignite hatred and jealousy in the forces of darkness and death in that community. God knows that jealous anger will conspire against life-giving Jesus to put him to death. Little did the powers of darkness know, this was all the plan of God to create a climactic showdown on the cross—between the breath-of-life-giving God, through Jesus Christ, and the darkness-yielding, breath-snatching Death?

In the fullness of God's timing, Jesus looks death and the devil in the face, recognizing the cup from which he must drink and submits himself to the will of God. He looks death in the face and says, "Let me have it." Death's forces arrest him and lead him from judgment hall to judgment hall. He endures their reviling and beating. He endures the condemnation of sinners on himself. He endures the cross, despising the shame. He endures the ridicule of the surrounding crowd, some of whom must have heard about his raising Lazarus from the very death to which he was seemingly about to succumb. He endures the betrayal of Judas, the denial of Peter, and the abandonment of his closest followers. He endures the sighs and tears of his own mother, as she witnesses his agony. He even endures a sense of disconnection from the God whom he declared "always hears."

Finally, when the time comes for Jesus to experience that breathlessness, he does not have his breath snatched from him. He does not have his life taken or stolen from him. When Jesus breathed his last breath from the cross, he declared with faith and confidence "Into thy hands I commit my breath." Understand, as Jesus yielded his spirit, exhaling from the cross, he knew that despite the agony, despite the condemnation, despite the ridicule, the pain, and the trauma, he would BREATHE AGAIN!

So, temporarily, Jesus enters the gates of death on Friday. Temporarily, he stays in the presence of death through Saturday. But, early on Sunday morning, Jesus, by the power of the Holy Spirit, BREATHES AGAIN. "I am he," Jesus said, "that lived and was dead, and behold me am alive forevermore." The testimony of the scripture is that, if the same Spirit, the same Breath, that raised Jesus from the dead, dwells in us, then, that same Spirit, that same Breath, will also make us alive. The very wind that life knocks out, God's Spirit breathes back in.

Now, my sisters and brothers, we are called to respond to the gospel of Jesus Christ with the activity of trusting faith. Knowing that Christ has defeated the power of death and breathlessness, gives us courage to face the tombs of our lives. We recognize that we don't have to be afraid, for whenever we see a tomb, we remember that, because of Christ, every tomb is temporary. Every tomb is temporary.

Observe the words of William Barclay's hymn as the answer to Toni Braxton's lament:

We praise Thee, O God!
For the Son of Thy love,
For Jesus Who died,
And is now gone above.
We praise Thee, O God!
For Thy Spirit of light,
Who hath shown us our Savior,
And scattered our night.
Refrain
All glory and praise
To the Lamb that was slain,
Who hath borne all our sins,
And hath cleansed every stain.
All glory and praise
To the God of all grace,
Who hast brought us, and sought us,
And guided our ways.
Revive us again;
Fill each heart with Thy love;
May each soul be rekindled
With fire from above.
Hallelujah! Thine the glory.
Hallelujah! Amen.
Hallelujah! Thine the glory.
Revive us again.

Thus, we ask our God to resurrect our love; resuscitate our faith; reinvigorate our hope; and restore our joy. Revive us, oh Lord. Let us breathe again!

" Ask For The Hard Thing "

A Sermon by CLAUDETTE A. COPELAND

*T*his message was preached at the closing session of the annual "Women in Ministry" Conference, Atlanta, Georgia. The focus was on young women who were finding their way (2008).

1 Kings 19:19-21 (New International Version)

So Elijah went from there and found Elisha son of Shaphat. He was plowing with twelve yoke of oxen and he himself was driving the twelfth pair. Elijah went up to him and threw his cloak around him. Elisha then left his oxen and ran after Elijah. "Let me kiss my father and mother good by," he said, "and then I will come after you." "Go back" Elijah replied. "What have I done to you?" So Elisha left him and went back. He took his yoke of oxen and slaughtered them. He burned the plowing equipment to

13

cook the meat and gave it to the people and they ate. Then
he set out to follow Elijah and became his attendant.

2 Kings 2:1-14 [verses 9-10 highlighted here]
(King James Version)

And it came to pass, when they were gone over that Elijah
said unto Elisha, "What shall I do for thee before I be taken
away from thee?' And Elisha said, "I pray thee, let a double
portion of thy spirit be upon me." And he said, Thou hast
asked a hard thing: nevertheless if thou see me when I am
taken away from thee, it shall be so unto thee..."

There will come a time when you will
become the woman that is inside you to become. The
landscape of your life will have changed before your
eyes. What will be the result? What demand will you
make on God, through the arrangements in your life?
How will you take hold, and traffic through the tasks
of maturing in faith that are given from the Lord?
Most importantly, what hunger has your studies in
the Word ignited in you?

Let us touch the text in four areas, as we reflect
on the reality of our readiness. You must decide if
you will take the path that leads to soundness, or
to superficiality, in the Gospel. You must decide if
you will opt for the "cute" or the things that make
for character. Will your goal be "ease" and public
exposure, or will you do the work of depth and
determination? Will you *ask for the hard thing?* For
you see, great callings incur great costs.

Where you discern great power in a woman,
there has been great pulverizing. A DOUBLE portion
of anointing demands a recurring decision to embrace

the "hard thing." It is an unfolding inheritance which begins with... a Meeting.

> *"So Elijah [the elder] went from there and found Elisha [the younger]...who was plowing with twelve yoke of oxen...and he went up to him and threw his cloak, [cast his mantle] upon him"* (I Kings 19: 19).

Some meetings are random, tangential, and apparently meaningless. Some contacts are, clearly, for the moment, unremembered and unmarked in your emotional history. The guy in the elevator, the woman you pass in the grocery store aisle, the maid who cleaned your room during your last travel; some meetings are for *moments.*

While some meetings are merely for moments, others are for your *making...* your movement towards your destiny. Think of that first teacher whose name you still remember after twenty-five years; or the first person you kissed, and *liked.* Think of the first love that broke your heart. Meetings have made you, corrected you, and failed you. Meetings have also made you stronger, shaped your view of life, and carved out your resolve to be a better person. Meetings may have motivated you to make one decision over the one not made.

There are even some meetings that are for our *misery.* Yes, along the way, there will be persons *sent by the evil one* to distract and detour you, to waste your time, to lie to you, and cause you to lose some sleep. These misery meetings are one of the enemy's tactics to seduce you away from your purpose and get you to enjoy disobedience. You may not believe it now, but some people want to hurt you, trip you, trouble you, insult you, even injure you. For no other reason except that they are on assignment from the devil. Now, since all things work together for your good, your misery meetings should leave you with a message, "Never allow, never embrace, or never do *that* thing again, ever!"

Some meetings are for the Master's eternal purposes. It was for the Tent of Meeting that Moses left the camp and went to commune with God, face to face (Exodus 33:11). Consider the meetings: the covenant you made in marriage, the first day you laid eyes on your newborn baby - moist, squirming, and fresh from your womb. Consider the first witness who spoke to you about your soul, or the first preacher who had a real word about your eternal destiny. The Master had an eternal purpose. There are and will be more meetings in your story. I beg you, *to make the meetings matter!*

God will place a spot light on your obscurity, causing people and events to seek you out. He will cause wise people to notice you and orchestrate ways for discerning men and women to put their eyes on you. You have to trust the plans of God for your life.

In 1 Kings 19:19, the older chooses the younger. The older sees and settles upon the protégée. God shows the younger to the older. "Go and anoint Elisha, a prophet in thy stead." He went from there and found Elisha.

God will always send you someone that is the teacher and/or mentor that is designed and designated by God to meet you unique needs. In the meantime, you must remember that although you might be broken, you are also bright. It may take time, but you are steady, tenacious, and unwilling to quit, God will send you-your Elijah. You may even be wounded, but keep the fire of "want-to" in your belly. Step up, and ask God for the hard thing!

Elijah threw his cloak around his mentee Elisha, and claimed Elisha for himself. "Come and follow me..." Maybe there is a young woman waiting to be claimed by you. A young soul in need of proper mentoring. She will not come uninvited. *Claim her*...she will not know how to come, or even that she needs to come.

There will be some meetings that God will arrange, that will radically call into question: WHAT ARE YOU DOING WITH YOUR LIFE? In the text, we see Elisha confronted with having to leave for his future and the longing for what he had always known. A little space of time will be allowed to consider and finish your business. You may go back for a moment, but do not keep God, nor Elijah, waiting too long.

Some meetings are designed to ignite *the slaying of your oxen,* and the saying goodbye to the secure places in and of your life. This will be a hard thing.

Then, the text suggests that there is the matter of the Miles. God will test your heart on the journey and will use the miles to do the testing. Maturity is not just quickly manifested... it is muddled toward, monitored, and made over time. Maturity, in life and in ministry, means to be "entire, wanting nothing, having readiness for re-productivity." Arriving there takes *miles*.

Elijah and Elisha. Ruth and Naomi. Jesus and The Twelve. There's a journey traveled together over a span of time. Months and miles, up close and personal. Behind the door, in unguarded moments is where a mentor can help develop maturity in a mentee. Do not be so quick to leave, abandon the process, and abort what is being developed. Elisha slew his oxen and burned his bridge to the past. He wholly pursued his destiny.

The final walk Elisha took with his mentor had a purpose which was not revealed until the walk was almost over. Sometimes you must walk through seasons, into revelation. Walk until the revelation becomes clear. Abram walked until God "showed him a land." Isaac walked from well to well until he found a place where his blessing would be unmolested by the Philistines. Sometimes the process of maturing takes miles. It is a hard journey to persevere through and reach the desired end.

Let's follow the children of Israel on a journey. Our starting place shall be Gilgal. The place of the wheel or circle, as well as the place where God has "rolled away their reproach." Gilgal is the first encampment that Joshua constructed, just after the children crossed Jordan. They pitched their tents in safety! They have won! They escaped, crossed over, and have taken hold of freedom and liberty. You will be tested, not just at hard places and in times of pain and problem. You will be tested at Gilgal, at the point of your *apparent victory*, when you seem to have gotten over and through and your battle is no longer raging. At the point when it seems the enemies have been drowned in the red sea and roaring lions have been reduced to carcasses, expect to face a test.

Coming from Gilgal, they have been together a long time now...Elijah and Elisha. It is in coming from the season of victory...that you become vulnerable. "Let he that thinks he stands, take heed, lest he fall." Elijah offers a stopping place: "Tarry here, at Gilgal." Elisha knows that if he is to see his desired end, he cannot let his mentor continue on without him. "No, I will not leave you. I am studying for the 'double portion," says the young mentee. There will be miles!

The next stop shall be Beth-el, House-of-God (WORSHIP). Genesis 28 reminds us that Elisha is directed to the place where Jacob had seen angels ascending and descending, where a pillar was set up and a vow was made. This was the place of worship. The hard thing is true worship—worship will expose truths about yourself. "I saw the Lord, high and lifted up...and I said woe is me," lamented Isaiah.

Before you can be entrusted with ministry, you must be entrusted with mirrors. Worship shows me *"me"*, in light of God's countenance. Worship at Bethel, the place of God, means an encounter with who God is and who I am *not*. *Hard things* are being asked of you and you are not even noticing. Come to the house of God (Bethel) and do not become seduced with platforms and pulpits, but come to worship. Do not become addicted to activity, a slave to mindless serving, and fail to worship. Some of us have become mere workers and are no longer worshippers! Preachers who do not PRAY are simply peddlers of the liturgy, having no personal revelation of worship.

Can you come from Gilgal and into Bethel? For a student of the "double portion" must walk miles. It is a hard thing to keep up, but if you choose the "miles," you will come to...Jericho. The teacher Elijah shows the student the necessity to touch the past as he prepares for the future.

Jericho (war): "Joshua fought the battle of Jericho, and the walls were tumbled down." Over the miles, we must appreciate what others have fought for in order that we might be here today! You must come to the terrain of Jericho, see it, survey it, and find the courage to fight for what is yours—the stuff the devil will not willingly relinquish. I hate a fight! I would rather make peace than war, but, inevitably, I am tested on my willingness to go to battle and fight instead of flee. You have to go in, uproot the things that are squatting on your land and put out the intruders who are blocking your inheritance.

From Jericho, the miles will lead us to Jordon, the place of crossing over together. The mentor must take the mentee as far as possible: open the waters for the youth, clear away paths for them, and hold their hands until they get to where they are supposed to be. Some things in life will happen while we are *together*. It is said that the greatness of a river is not how wide it is or how deep it is alone; the greatness of a river, is in the tributaries that it spawns. Watch closely! Lessons are being pressed out for you to embrace and miracles are being manifested for you to witness… all while we are together. This is the preparing of the youth to rise and take over the positions we have carved out in the world.

Elijah rolls up his mantle, and parts the waters one last time! So, finally, after many meetings and many miles, comes the matter of *the mantle*. The mantle represents the authority and the pre-eminence. There is one mantle *placed early on* Elisha, the student. However, there is a very different mantle that Elisha, the prophet, must *pick up* himself if he is to succeed in his own future.

Elijah, the teacher, has modeled the lesson of mentoring: "I can prepare you… but I cannot possess you." At each point he gives the younger the option to stop here. Elisha, the student, passed the test of tenacity—his purpose was to mature, and to master each of life's lessons. Elisha stuck to his teacher, traveled where he was not forced to go, all in order to gain the lessons he did not know he would need.

Do you have relationships wit some mileage on them that are preparing you for your mantle of leadership? Do you have teachers who are expanding your horizons, taking you to new places? Are you reaching or are you resisting? Is there always a… "Yes, *but*…?" There is a mantle specifically for you, but picking it up will be the hard thing.

Once you cross over your Jordan, you will have to tear your old clothes, and pick up a new identity. YOU must pick up the mantle that has fallen from *your* Elijah. What are you asking for while your mentors are among you? Let it be the hard thing: "I want to inherit a double portion of your spirit."

Then, comes the Ministry. The student has been juxtaposed between leaving and being left, learning and longing. In 2 Kings 2:12, "As they were walking along still," two words appear in the NIV: *suddenly* and *separated*. You do not know when life will ring the door bell and say, "Special delivery! Tag, you're it." The senior pastor may leave or die, and… tag, you're it! A position will become vacant, a microphone will await a voice of reason, or a defense will need to be mounted, and… *you're it.*

Elisha asks for the hard thing—the spirit that was on his mentor, in double measure. On the other side of Jordan, he picks up the mantle, and strikes the water for himself and it divided to the right and the left. What is the point? The stuff you are taught has got to work for *YOU*. The "hard thing" is not the miracle. The hard thing is being prepared for God to use you for the manifestation of the miracle. The hard thing is not getting the "fire to fall" on your altar. The hard thing is to rightly prepare the altars in your life, so that you will be God's woman in the face of Mt. Carmel.

The hard thing is not the winning of souls, and detouring them from hell, or the disciplining of the wayward. The hard thing is to bring *your own soul* under subjection to the making of the master. The challenge is to endure hardness as a good soldier of Jesus Christ; to fight the fatigue factor, and to live the liturgy that you preach! The hard thing is *not* "finishing well" at the crucifixion. The hard thing is the Garden of Gethsemane, where the eternal "Yes, Lord" must be decided. This is the place where coming to an unyielding decision that you only want the will of the Lord to be done in your life.

There are meetings which will prepare you, miles which will shape you and mantles that will fall on you through the sovereignty of God. Then, there are the decisions which, by grace, you must continue to make. Pick up the mantle! Ask for the hard thing so you will be fully prepared and furnished for every good work. The waters will part before you! The ax heads will float!

"And ELISHA did twice as many miracles as his teacher." Ask for the hard thing! Amen.

"You Can Overcome It"

A Sermon by SHELETA FOMBY

Numbers 13:26-33 (New Living Translation)

To Moses, Aaron, and the whole community of Israel at Kadesh in the wilderness of Paran. They reported to the whole community what they had seen and showed them the fruit they had taken from the land. This was their report to Moses: "We entered the land you sent us to explore, and it is indeed a bountiful country—a land flowing with milk and honey. Here is the kind of fruit it produces. But the people living there are powerful, and their towns are large and fortified. We even saw giants there, the descendants of Anak! The Amalekites live in the Negev, and the Hittites, Jebusites, and Amorites live in the hill country. The Canaanites live along the coast of the Mediterranean Sea and along the Jordan Valley." But Caleb tried to quiet the people as they stood before Moses. "Let's go at once to take the land," he said. "We *can certainly conquer it!"   But the other men who had explored the land with him disagreed. "We can't go up against them! They are stronger than we are!" So they spread this bad report about the land among the Israelites: "The land we traveled through and explored will devour anyone who goes to live there. All the people we saw were huge. We even saw giants there, the descendants of Anak. Next to them we felt like grasshoppers, and that's what they thought, too!"*

As believers and children of the Most High God, we hold to the fundamental conviction that we walk by faith and not by sight. Our internal security in the faithfulness of God is not influenced, nor is it impacted, by what we see going on around us. Yet, the enemy of our soul, Satan himself, tries to pull us out of the realm of faith and into the realm of fear, by stealing our focus and distorting our perspective. He co-opts our internal thinking, in order to effect how we interpret our external reality.

What our enemy fails to understand, is that no matter how much he huffs and puffs, whenever God has made a promise —no demon in hell can take it away. You must understand that the enemy has no real authority to withhold anything that God has promised you. The God we serve is not only a promise maker, but He's also a promise keeper. So, what the enemy does, since he knows our future in God is already fixed, is try to influence our minds, in order to distort our *perception* of that promise. He uses every wicked weapon in his arsenal to keep us from maximizing our faith and being over-comers through Christ Jesus our Lord. He uses anxiety, depression, fear and he attacks and assaults our self-worth and self-esteem. The enemy comes against our self-confidence, and tries to destroy our confidence in God. Then, if all that fails, he resorts to the demonic device of intimidation.

It reminds me of my one and only fight in life. I'll never forget being terrorized and terrified as a child by a neighborhood bully. I remember, at the age of 12, being intimidated by a young lady who was bigger, older, and taller than me. For an entire school year, I lived under the threat of intimidation, only to find out later that just one punch to the stomach was all it took to remedy the situation. While that's not the *proudest* moment of my life, it was in fact a very *profound* one. What I discovered was, for too long, I was afraid of something that I already had enough strength to defeat. I discovered that intimidation had crippled me from doing something that I had the power to do long ago.

If I would have done, at the beginning of the year, what I found the courage to do at the end of year, I could have saved myself a lot of time, tears, and trouble. I wonder how different your life would look, how much further along would you be right now, if you had not let the market bully you out of buying the house, if the threat of failing had not bullied you out of applying for the degree, if you had not let the threat of competition stop you from answering your call to ministry.

Now, you find yourself still marking time, bewildered in the wilderness of life, because you've allowed the enemy to punk you out of the lunch money of your blessings. When will you no longer regress and retreat, but stand up, assume your rightful position in the kingdom of God, and say, "alright devil, if it's a fight you want, then I'll see you at 3:00."

I can no longer afford to delay my destiny by majoring in the minors and matriculating in the mundane. I have a great and marvelous inheritance waiting on me, and I'm going do everything in my power to possess the promises of God for my life. For God has not given us a spirit of fear, but of power, love and a sound mind.

This is what was taking place in the text. The Bible says that the Israelites were under the oppressive heel of the Egyptians for 400 years, forced to make bricks without of straw. Their cries and lament came up before the Lord, and God remembered Israel saying, "I see, I hear, I know and I'm coming down to deliver." I'm so glad the God we serve is not so high and lifted up, or so transcendent, that he can't come down and meet us at the very point of need. Isn't it exciting to know that, even if no one else understands, God will hear your faintest cry and He'll answer by and by?

The Bible says that God raised up Moses as an agent of deliverance, and, in the fullness of time, he delivered his people out of the land of Egypt—out of the house of bondage. God created a highway in the middle of the sea, put the water up as walls on both sides, so that the children of Israel could pass through the Red Sea on dry land. He brought them out of Egypt into Canaan, but first, they had to sojourn through the wilderness. Understand, just because God brings you out to take you in, that it doesn't mean you will never have to go through further tests.

The Israelites had to journey through the inhospitable terrain of the wilderness, and, even though God had brought them out of Egypt, the challenge was getting the Egypt out of them. You know how it is when you are no longer in a certain environment, yet that environment is still in you? The transition can be difficult, because a change of venue does not always equate to a change of values. They were free circumstantially, but still bound cerebrally by a slave mentality. The Bible says that despite his marvelous acts of deliverance, the Israelites refused to turn their hearts toward God, and they complained and murmured against God and Moses.

So, due to their stubbornness and recal-citrance, the Israelites were delayed in the wilderness until they could learn how depend on God. Now, may I tell you the reason some of you are still in a holding pattern—circling the perimeter of your purpose? It is not because you're not gifted. It is not because you're not competent or capable. It is because you just have a nasty attitude. Deliver me, please, from Christians who are chronic complainers, despite how good, gracious, and generous God has been. Like the Children of Israel, you still find ought and opportunity to complain about what God has not done for you. Despite the fact that He woke you up this morning, started you on your way, put money in your pocket, a roof over your head and clothes on your back, you still complain. God is so good to us, but too often we murmur and come into His holy presence with legs crossed and arms folded, as if praise were a matter of prerogative.

It was because of God's goodness that He said, "Look, I'm going to give you another opportunity to leave this place and go into the Promised Land." So, He told Moses to appoint twelve men, one from each of the twelve tribes, to go spy out the Land of Canaan. After a sufficient time of observation and evaluation, they returned and, of the twelve spies that were dispatched, ten of them returned with a report that was contrary to God's promise. They said, "We've seen the abundance, and the land is indeed overflowing with milk and honey, but that's not the only thing that's over there. There are giants in the land, from the descendants of Anak!" They concluded that, based on how intimidating the situation looked, they would not go in and possess the promise. For they said, "there are giants there, and we appear as grasshoppers in our own sight."

That's exactly what intimidation will do. It will impair *your vision* and cause you to see the obstacle before you see the opportunity. Although the land was fruitful and fertile, all they could see was that the land was already occupied. Oft times, we let the enemy distort our vision because we magnify the strength of the giants over and against the strength of our God. Whenever you lift a man's attributes higher than the authority of God's Word, you will always see yourself as inferior and inadequate.

The Israelites were discouraged because when they arrived at the place of their blessing, the land was already occupied by giants. What they failed to understand is, just because someone is already in the position, it does not nullify the blessing spoken by God. The point is, position doesn't always equal possession. No, I am not intimidated because you have the position. I understand that the possession belongs to whoever has the promise!

In other words, just because someone else is already in it doesn't mean they own it. The earth is the Lord's, and the fullness thereof. That's a word of encouragement for someone reading this message. You have been feeling threatened by someone's position in the church, in the community, or in the congregation. You have allowed them to intimidate you and keep you from assuming your rightful place in God, because they've been there longer than you. Understand that just because you have a multiplicity of numbers behind your tenure, and a multiplicity of numbers behind your age, that doesn't qualify you for the position. The anointing is what qualifies you. There's an inherent difference between being anointed *for* a position and being appointed *to* a position.

Some people have gotten where they are based on the strength of their giant bank account, giant title, or giant credentials, connections and certifications. Then, there are those who, even though they may have the education of a grasshopper, the skills of a grasshopper, the looks of a grasshopper, and the experience of a grasshopper, the one thing you do have working for them is that they serve a giant-sized God! I don't care how big their reputation is or how big their station and standing is, promotion doesn't come from the east nor the west, from the north nor the south. Promotion comes from God.

In other words, someone other than you may have the advantage, but with God you have the authority. That's why David told Goliath, you come to me in the strength of the javelin, the sword and the spear; but I come to you in the name of the Lord. For the name of the Lord is a strong tower, the righteous run therein and are safe."

Now that's an interesting statement because the text never said that the giants were ever aware of the presence of the Israelites. I mean, we don't see where the giants ever spoke, noticed, or acknowledged them at all. However, that's what the spirit of intimidation does. Not only does it cause you to exaggerate what you see, but it skews your perspective on how you see what you see.

In other words, because they saw themselves as grasshoppers, they assumed the giants saw them in the same way. The reality is: all of us know people who are that way. Everyone knows someone who is so paranoid with his/her own insecurity that they assume everyone else is looking at them funny. When the truth of the matter is no one is paying them any attention at all.

I've gotten to the point where I really don't have time to expend the energy worrying about how I look in someone else's eyes. And if I were you I wouldn't waste another minute of time living life by committee. I mean, who cares how other people view you - *they* didn't die for you, *they* didn't save you, *they* didn't redeem you, and *they* didn't call you. No, instead of worrying how you look to everyone else, you ought to be running with endurance the race that has been set before you. "Fixing your eyes on Jesus, the author and finisher of your faith." At the end of the day, the only opinion that matters is what God thinks about you, whether God is pleased with you and how you look in *His* eyes!

The Israelites were intimidated by the giants, but they were also afraid of something else. I believe that, in addition to the giants, they were also intimidated by the unknown. They had been in bondage for so long that, even though it was oppressive, it was still familiar. While in the wilderness, God provided for their every need. They were given manna for their daily bread, clothes that did not wear out, and shoes that did not wax over. He provided a pillar of cloud by day and a pillar of fire by night. At that point, the Israelites were now, however, graduating to another level of blessing and sustenance. So, not only were they threatened by how big the giants were, but they were also intimidated by how big the promotion, or the opportunity, was.

God is calling you to do some *big* things, but you're scared half to death, because you feel as though the opportunity is too great for you. God wants to elevate you and *take* you to places you've never been before. He's trying to take you to another level in your ministry, in your finances, in your marriage, and in your faith. You are the one who won't go in and possess the promise, because you're afraid of the unknown responsibility that comes with it. You're too worried about whether you can handle the vast new responsibility. The reality is, it's none of your business, it's God's business. It's His job to supply every one of your needs, all you have to do is "trust in the Lord with all your heart and lean not to your own understanding, but in all your ways acknowledge Him, and watch God direct your path." If the Lord clothed the birds of the air and the lilies of the field, how much more will He care for one in His likeness? See, your problem is not one of *competence*; it's, rather, one of *confidence*. Paul said, "if you don't do anything else, be confident of this very thing: He who has begun a good work in you, will fulfill it until the day of Christ." Stop worrying and just start walking, because while you're trying to figure it out, God has already worked it out.

The Bible says they were so scared that intimidation began to infect and infest their conversation. The children of Israel said, "would that we had died in the land of Egypt," because they feared the future more than they trusted God. They took a vote to go back to Egypt and return to bondage. They said, "at least there we had fish, melons, leeks, onions, and garlic."

Understand that whenever you're afraid of the unknown, the enemy will always tempt you with something that's *familiar*—even if it has the potential to be *fatal*. This is a word of warning for someone who is at a crossroads of conscious decision-making. Whether you're going forward with God, or returning back to Egypt. Heed the Word of the Lord, "if you return, it's going to be seven times worse than it was before. For how long will you halt between two decisions? Choose ye this day who you will serve. God is calling you to higher, holier levels of living."

I'm talking to some woman who's thinking about going back to an *abusive* relationship. I'm talking to some young man who's been tempted to go back to selling on the corner. I'm talking to the husband thinking of returning to that addiction of pornography and licentious living. God snatched you out of it once—be not entangled with that bondage again. For, if any person puts his hand to the plow and looks back, he's not fit for the kingdom. I can't speak for anyone else, but I made up in my mind, as for me and my house we will serve the Lord. I've been there, I've done that, and Egypt doesn't have anything I want. So, come hell, or demonic high-water, I'm not going back into the bondage of depression, the bondage of debt, the bondage of discouragement, or the bondage of low self-esteem.

The Bible says those Israelites were paralyzed by fear, because they were too saved to go back yet to scared to go forward. But Joshua and Caleb spoke out and said, "look everyone settle down. I know the situation looks intimidating but *we are well able to overcome it.*"

That's really all I want to say: tell someone, when the devil is threatening you and trying to intimidate you out of your inheritance in God for you can't just sit there and be quiet. The only way you're going to survive the attack of intimidation is to learn to talk back to that demon! The power is not in what you see, but the power is in what you *say* to what you see. All twelve of the spies saw the same threat, but Joshua and Caleb were the only two to declare the promises of God. That is significant, because the issue is not that you see the giants, the issue is what you say to the giants you see.

Look at your Giants, and then look at your God, and say, "I am well able to overcome it, because

I can do all things through Christ who strengthens me." Learn to open your mouth and declare and decree that greater is He that's in me than he that's in the world.

When the boss threatens to fire you, don't be intimidated. Just say to your boss, I am well able to overcome it because God shall supply all my needs according to his riches in glory. Fret not when the economy intimidates you with bankruptcy, just declare that you are well able to overcome it, because I've never seen the righteous forsaken nor his seed begging bread.

Get up in the morning, square your shoulders, look in the mirror, and tell yourself, "I am fearfully and wonderfully made." Open your mouth and begin to talk back to intimidation, because life and death is in the power of the tongue. When disease is intimidating you, remember, you can overcome it, because He was wounded for our transgression and by His stripes you are healed.

The reason Caleb and Joshua could speak with a confident boldness is because victory was in their blood. Caleb comes from the tribe of Judah, which means praise, and the only way you can be free of the spirit of intimidation, fear, dread and anxiety is by exchanging that spirit of heaviness for a garment of praise. The only way the enemy can intimidate you out of your promise is, if you let him intimidate you out of your praise! Joshua's name comes from the Hebrew word Jeshua which means, "Yahweh is salvation." So, why are you afraid when you've already been saved from what's trying to defeat you? No, you don't have to wait until the battle is over.

You can shout right now, knowing that no weapon formed against you shall be able to prosper. I'm saved by His glory divine and saved to a new life sublime; life is now sweet, and my joy is complete. I am saved, saved, saved! No matter what the giants are in your life, take courage and know You are Well Able to Overcome It!

"Organ Donor"

A Sermon by CECELIA E. GREENEBARR

*T*he following sermon was preached at New Hope Missionary Baptist Church in Southfield, MI for their 2009 Women's Day Service. The theme of their women's service was, "Confident Women Empowered by God."

Psalm 40:1-11 (New Living Translation)

I waited patiently for the Lord to help me, and he turned to me and heard my cry. He lifted me out of the pit of despair, out of the mud and the mire. He set my feet on solid ground and steadied me as I walked along. He has given me a new song to sing, a hymn of praise to our God. Many will see what he has done and be amazed. They will put their trust in the Lord. Oh, the joys of those who trust the Lord, who have no confidence in the proud or in those who worship idols. O Lord my God, you have performed many wonders for us. Your plans for us are too numerous to list. You have no equal. If I tried to recite all your wonderful deeds, I would never come to the end of them. You take no delight in sacrifices or offerings. Now that you have made me listen, I finally understand - you don't require burnt offerings or sin offerings. Then I said, "Look, I have come. As is written about me in the Scriptures: I take joy in doing your will, my God, for your instructions are written on my heart." I have told all your people about your justice. I have not been afraid to speak out, as you, O Lord, well know. I have not kept the good news of your justice hidden in my heart; I have talked about your faithfulness and saving power. I have told everyone in the great assembly of your unfailing love and faithfulness. Lord, don't hold back your tender mercies from me. Let your unfailing love and faithfulness always protect me.

Of all the systems or organs in the body, it is the heart that we think of in terms of our strengths or weaknesses. In the old comedy show *Sanford and Son*, Redd Foxx was known for the climatic moment of grabbing his chest, calling for his dearly departed Elizabeth, and motioning as if his heart was about to give out at any second. Sometimes we say people don't have the heart to make tough decisions. We've even had moments when we've had to admit that we didn't have the heart to disappoint someone. For some of us the empowerment that we need cannot be found in a six-week course in assertiveness. I suspect that the empowerment that some of us need is not another promotion on our jobs, more in our bank accounts, or greater political affiliation. But, I suspect on this day that the empowerment that some of us need is a new heart!

Several years ago, my family had the experience of walking alongside a relative as she was diagnosed with a failing heart. She was told she would need a transplant in order to continue living. It did not matter that she had a history of being a cigarette smoker. Nor did it matter that she had not given her body the best chance at health through regular physical exercise. None of that really mattered at that moment. What mattered at that moment was that if she was going to continue living she would need a new heart. If hearing the news was not enough to take the wind out of everyone's sails, we then learned that the process of receiving a heart from the exact type of donor was not predictable. She never knew when an organ would become available. She didn't know if the donor organ would be accepted or rejected by her system once it was transplanted. All she knew was that the heart she had was no longer healthy enough to maintain a quality life. That which was within her heart was no longer life-giving, but life depleting. She needed a new heart. If there were one compelling biblical example of someone who had to examine the health of his heart, and the heart of the congregation, it was David.

In the fortieth Psalm we are listening in on a conversation that David is having with God, as he confesses his past history with the Lord. If you want to know the health of your heart, the health of your friend's heart, or even the health of your church I suggest you start by looking at accounts of past history with the Lord. What do your life past accounts look like in comparison to even yesterday? What do I mean by past? I mean before salvation, before consecration, before you were baptized, before you were filled with the Holy Spirit with evidence of speaking in tongues...past! Before you became a deacon, an usher, or had any title at all in the church—that's what I mean by *past*. If your past interactions look like yesterday's interactions, then perhaps your heart is no longer healthy. Maybe this would be a good time to check in with the great physician for a thorough examination of the health of your heart.

David testifies about the benefits of waiting patiently for the Lord. This is one area where so many believers can examine their ability to wait patiently for the Lord. David wants us to know that waiting patiently for the Lord does not guarantee the absence of tribulation. Waiting patiently for the Lord does not mean that you will not have some down days and some disappointments. It does not mean that you will not get a bad report from the doctor when you were not expecting it. It does not mean that open doors of opportunity will be extended to you when you really do desire it. Waiting patiently for the Lord does not even guarantee that the enemies of our soul will be destroyed the very moment we call on Him. Waiting patiently for the Lord means that you just have to learn how to wait! Patience deals with our attitude while we are waiting.

David testified that waiting patiently for the Lord resulted in the Lord activating spiritual blessings for him. Blessing number one: God inclined his ear to David and heard his cry. Blessing number two: God lifted David from a desolate place. Blessing number three: God established David. Blessing number four: God gave David songs to sing. Blessing number five: David becomes a witness for the Lord. Blessing number six: David is happy because he discovered that God can be trusted. Blessing number seven: David has discernment to see what God has been doing all along. Blessing number eight: David received revelation that no one can compare with the Lord. Blessing number nine: God has given David an opened ear. In other words, God has given David access. You know, sometimes all we really want is for God to hear our cry. Isn't that what we want, for God to give us access? Even if your situation remains the same after you've finished praying and fasting, doesn't it soothe your soul when you discern that your petitions have been heard?

Church, the message I hope we can clearly see in this passage—is what God did for David once he decided to wait patiently on the Lord. The message I hope we can see in this passage is that David allowed what God had done for him to make a change in him. It's wonderful what God does for us. But, have we allowed what we've seen God do in our lives to make a change in us? You can pray all day long for God to open the windows of heaven and pour you out a blessing that you do not have room enough to receive. God may turn around and answer your prayer, and you still maintain a rancid attitude. You can pray all day long for God to give you the mate you want. God may turn around and answer your prayer, but your selfishness doesn't seem to change. So, you can't hold on to the blessings God gives. You can pray all day long for God to give you favor. And God surprises you and surrounds you with favor. You look like you have The Midas Touch. Yet, you are so two-faced, that all you do is step on people instead of lifting them up. You can pray all day long for God to give you divine health for a long life. And yet, you go out and do despicable things with your body not recognizing that your body is the temple of the Most High God. It's not so much about what God is able to do, church, it's about whether or not we are willing to let what God does create a change within us. It's not about the availability or potency of God's power, it's about the condition of our hearts. How many of us are willing and interested in having our hearts changed?

May I suggest to us today that David's heart, at one point, was not very healthy? Oh sure, he wrestled bears and lions. David could work a full day in the fields and he could even sing and play instruments. David's heart could perform routine activities, but it was not healthy enough to perform the ridiculously audacious feats that God was calling him to perform. I believe we know when God is calling us to perform great exploits for the Him. God calls us to perform ridiculously audacious feats that require a heart that is not stuck in miry clay. This requires a heart *not* stuck on pettiness. God is calling a people who have a heart that can do great exploits. Sure, your heart is healthy enough to show up for Sunday worship. You might even be healthy enough to hang-in for an occasional all night prayer service, but that is the extent of it. But is your heart healthy enough to be stretched by miracles you cannot explain? Is it healthy enough to make unpopular decisions—that align your life with the Word instead of social commentary? David allowed God to take his old heart and replace it with a new heart.

How do you know God gave David a new heart? Listen to how David's confession changes. He starts out in a desolate pit and ends up with God's law in his heart. He starts out calling God for help, and ends up proclaiming to the congregation the greatness of the Lord. Church, something happened to David that changed his heart. Somewhere between being a shepherd boy and hiding in a cave from Saul's attacks, David's heart changed. Somewhere between plotting Uriah's death and Absalom's uprising, David's heart changed. Somewhere between loving Bathsheba and Tamar being raped, David's heart changed. Somewhere between having prophecy spoken over his life and later reigning as king, David's heart changed. Somewhere between your bad days and your good days, there should be a change in your heart. Somewhere between being out there working for the devil and being in church holding up hands, there should be a change in your heart.

Allow me to close here with an epilogue on my cousin's condition. She received a new organ and her body did not reject the procedure. The experience was so transformational that she created a new email address, "second at life," just to communicate to everyone what God had done on her behalf. She was very much aware that someone had to die in order for the heart to have been donated, which gave her a second chance at life. Although she knew someone had died, she was clear to give God thanks for her second chance at life.

David, on the other hand, didn't have the internet as a means to tell everyone what God had done in his life and in his heart, so he used what he had available. David spoke and did not hide what God had been done for him. David was fully aware of the law that said that blood had to be shed for the remission of sins. And still, David knew the magnitude of his sins and that he was unworthy for all that God had done for him. David must have thought to himself, I don't deserve it, but God has changed me. David declared that he couldn't keep the testimony of God's graciousness to himself. David must have thought, "This kind of redemption I can't keep to myself!" This kind of help...I can't keep to myself.

Church, I don't know what you are going through today. I do not know the health of your heart today. Maybe you are thinking that you are too far in sin for God to give you a new heart. Maybe you are thinking that you are no good. Maybe you are thinking your mind is no good or your attitude is no good. But, I have good news today for the person who feels they are too far into the grip of sin. Someone has already died in order that you may live. His name is Jesus! Jesus has died so that you might have an entirely new heart. Don't stand around with your head hung low, lift up your head, and cry out to God, "Lord create in me a clean heart."

David could have rejected what God gave him, but for all of us today I can hear David saying, "God has entered my heart and I am changed." I live because of God's faithfulness. I live because of God's love. I live because of God's saving grace. I live because God delivered me. I live because God helped me. I live because God gave me what I could not give myself—another heart. Not a heart of facts, not a heart of information, not a heart of programmed habits, not a heart of logic…nor a heart of ideas. God entered my heart and now I'm changed. God gave me a new mind. I looked at my hands and they are new. I've evaluated my dreams and they are new dreams too.

The Spirit of the Lord is here to give you a new heart. David said, "You live in my heart." Can I tell you that where God dwells, He lives large. He lives large enough to push back the darkness. He lives large enough to overshadow doubts. He lives large enough to expose His own faithfulness. He lives large enough to cover my worries and fears. He lives large enough that even if I didn't want to tell of His goodness, I still couldn't keep it to myself. Why is that? I'll tell you why, it's because God lives within my heart today.

"The Secret to Your Success"

A Sermon by CYNTHIA L. HALE

Joshua 1:1-9 (New Living Translation)

*A*fter the death of Moses the Lord's servant, the Lord spoke to Joshua son of Nun, Moses' assistant. He said, "Moses my servant is dead. Therefore, the time has come for you to lead these people, the Israelites, across the Jordan River into the land I am giving them. I promise you what I promised Moses: 'Wherever you set foot, you will be on land I have given you— from the Negev wilderness in the south to the Lebanon mountains in the north, from the Euphrates River in the east to the Mediterranean Sea in the west, including all the land of the Hittites.' No one will be able to stand against you as long as you live. For I will be with you as I was with Moses. I will not fail you or abandon you. "Be strong and courageous, for you are the one who will lead these people to possess all the land I swore to their ancestors I would give them. Be strong and very courageous. Be* *careful to obey all the instructions Moses gave you. Do not deviate from them, turning either to the right or to the left. Then you will be successful in everything you do. Study this Book of Instruction continually. Meditate on it day and night so you will be sure to obey everything written in it. Only then will you prosper and succeed in all you do. This is my command—be strong and courageous! Do not be afraid or discouraged. For the Lord your God is with you wherever you go."*

What is your ambition in life? What do you hope to achieve? What legacy do you intend to leave behind? When history is written, what do you want it to say about you? Every one of us has the capacity to be a success, to accomplish great things, and to push pass the limits we and others have placed on us with their ideas of what is possible for us. Isn't it interesting how people always seem to have the inside scoop on what we are capable of, and what we can accomplish given what they view as our strengths and weaknesses, abilities, and resources?

What is also interesting to me is how much weight we give to the critiques of others. What do they know? They didn't create us; they have no clue about all God has invested in you, and what He has in store for you. All they have are their opinions. We dare not determine what is possible in our lives on the opinions of others or even our own at times.

We don't always take ourselves and our abilities as seriously as we should. We tend to down play who we are. We fail to realize the full extent of our possibilities while settling for less than the best and doing just enough to get by.

You had better get a grip. When you became a Christian, you entered into a whole new realm of opportunity and possibility. There isn't anything in line with God's plan and purpose for your life that you can't achieve. What seems impossible in the natural is exactly what God wants to do for you supernaturally. As a matter of fact, it is God's will and desire that you prosper and succeed in every way (Jeremiah 29:11).

The Psalmist, David, understood the magnitude of our potential, for he penned in Psalms 40:5, *"Many, O lord my God, are the wonders you have done. The things you planned for us no one can recount to you; were I to speak and tell of them, they would be too many to declare."*

Before the foundation of the world, God put a plan in place for your life as a promissory note that insures you of success, a road map, if you will, to lead you into your destiny. God created us with the capacity to excel. The sky is the limit for what we can be and do. There is a plan for your life, and success is guaranteed, so what are you waiting for? What is holding you back?

All you have to do is dare to dream of what is possible. Dreams or visions are the means by which God reveals to us what He has in store for us. My friend, Claudette A. Copeland says, "A vision is a snapshot of your future seen through the eyes of faith." God drops into our spirits, the seed of an idea that has to be taken seriously in order for it to become reality.

Once you have the vision, you must write it, develop your own personal plan to achieve it, and then work the plan. Some of you have a plan in place but you still aren't moving. What's the problem?

Are you afraid that you cannot achieve what is in your heart and mind? Are you afraid that you can't live up to the expectations of others, or afraid that you will fail? Any mistakes that we view as failures, are actually opportunities to learn what not to do the next time, and advance us to the next step. Those missteps that we view as set-backs are really set-ups that God uses to launch us into the unlimited possibilities that are before us.

Becoming a success is really not as difficult as some of us might want to believe given the fact that we are twice born in Christ. Each of us has not only been created with purpose and potential beyond our wildest imagination, but we are also heirs of the promise. We are the seed of Abraham. The blessings that God promised Him are now ours through faith in Christ. With faith, nothing is impossible to us!

So, what is it you want to do—start your own a business, develop a school, write a book, produce a major record label, or win a record deal? Would you like to have own T.V. show or studio, become a doctor, a lawyer, a journalist, a teacher, a preacher, an entrepreneur, a world-class athlete, author, or an artist? What is it that you are uniquely created for—that thing that only you can achieve given your gift mix, your personality, your intellect, and your passion?

I know you would like to have the assurance that whatever you attempt will be achieved with the greatest of ease. You want to be confident that what you're going after will come to pass. You want to make sure that you are doing all the right things to get you to where you are trying to go. Like most folks, you want to know if there is a secret to success.

Of course there is, the world would say, as they tell you that it is not what you know but who you know, indicating that you have to know the right folks, network, and get connected with a specific crew. Others would say you have to get in with the boss if you are seeking a promotion, or impress someone who can drop your name or write a recommendation for you.

The secret to success for the world and the Kingdom-minded are quite different; because in the Kingdom, success and prosperity are also defined differently. You see, success in the world is defined as having position, power, wealth, and fame. Whereas, success in the Kingdom is defined as discovering your destiny, fulfilling your purpose, pleasing God and bringing glory to Him through serving others. Being a success is making a difference in the world and in the lives of its people, as only you are uniquely qualified to do.

When you have this kind of success, then the material things are not as important. But, God usually throws them in as a bonus; a reward for doing it His way. The secret of success is doing it God's way! Let me show you what that means. In the Old Testament book of Joshua, God outlines for Joshua the secret of success for the people of God. God actually gives

Joshua a roadmap into their destiny as he and the people of Israel stand at the edge of their promised blessing.

Like you and I, Israel had the world before them, unlimited possibilities at their fingertips, a divine destiny that was enviable, and God's promise of prosperity staring them in the face—only a few steps away, literally. The parameters of the promise were mind-blowing; almost too good to be true. If we were talking about anyone else, it would be unbelievable. But, you know that God has a heart for His people. He is madly in love with us, and nothing is too good for His beloved; we are all the apple of His eye.

God enjoys blessing us with the best and nothing less. So, the promises He made to Israel are the essence of what He promises all who live in covenant relationship with Him and walk upright. The Psalmist says in 84:11, *"No good thing does he withhold from those whose walk is blameless."* As He prepares Joshua for the mammoth task of leading the people into their destiny, He reminds them of three promises that He had already given them through Moses.

The first promise is that of a secured possession. In verse 23, *"Now then you and all these people get ready to cross the Jordan River into the land I am about to give to them – to the Israelites. I will give you every place where you set your foot."* Every place you set your foot will be yours.

God had already given them the land of Canaan. It had already been promised to them, they just had to go in and claim it. They would claim the land by "walking" on it.

They could have as much as they were willing to walk on, which meant that if there were any limitations, it would be self-imposed. If they didn't get as much land as they wanted, it wouldn't be anyone's fault but theirs. There was no limit to what they could have; the land was wide open. They just had to claim it. They had to make their way prosperous.

The same is true for us! The promises God has made to us, make the possibilities for our lives wide open. The sky is the limit to what we can have and do. God promises and what God speaks, is already done, secured, and assured. Having the promise of God concerning something is as good as having it in your hand. We just have to claim it by faith!

The problem is we limit what we can have and do by our lack of faith. We don't trust God to do what He says He will do. Furthermore, the faith that we claim to have lies dormant most of the time, and we don't put it to work. We talk it, but we don't walk it. The Bible says, "Faith without works is dead." We have to claim what is already ours by faith and give practical evidence of our faith by walking in it, pursuing it, and going after it; *you will never possess what you will not pursue.*

Now, this is problematic for some of us because we are lazy, too laid back, unmotivated, passive, sitting back waiting for someone to give it to us or for it to fall out of the sky. God does not open the windows of heaven and pour out a blessing until after we do what He says we are to do. We have to trust and obey the Word of God. Claiming what is ours takes effort. Walking the land is a faith walk, but it is also some work. God said that they could have whatever they walked on. I am afraid that the reason many of us have not moved on God's purpose for us is that we want God to do all the work. We want God to perform a miracle and beam us into our destiny. We do not want to do all that is involved in becoming successful.

Practically speaking, being successful requires hard work, planning, sacrifice, discipline and perseverance, especially when you are starting your own business or trying to establish yourself in your area of expertise in corporate and non-profit circles. For some of us it will mean, going back to school, or staying in school and graduating. Some of you don't have the luxury of quitting your job to go to school; you will have to work and go to school. Much energy has to be expended to become successful at anything.

Too many of us spend a lot of time dreaming, but our dreams never get realized! The promise of God is this: "everywhere you place your feet, when you expend your time and energy...I will make it worth your while."

Several years ago, Ray of Hope was outgrowing its building and we needed to move or expand. We were struggling with whether we were to build or buy existing property. When the Lord showed us the possibility of buying New Birth Missionary Baptist Church, I wasn't sure we could do it. The campus had four buildings compared to our one. The sanctuary seated 10 times the number that our present building seated.

I invited the people to join me at the building one morning at 6:00 am to walk the grounds. We walked that land and claimed it by faith. The Bishop called and offered to sell it. The next day, the bank called and offered to fund the purchase, and we were able to buy the building. But, that was not all we had to do. We had to raise the down payment, complete the loan requirements to qualify for the loan, close the deal, and move in.

The second promise God made is that of unending protection (verse 5), "No one will be able to stand up against you all the days of your life." The way we know that we are in line with God's will and purpose for our lives is that there is opposition from the enemy who often uses people, circumstances, and situations in our lives. He attacks our faith, our confidence in ourselves, our character, and our resources—whatever it is that will cause us to give up and retreat.

The land of Canaan was already inhabited with people that God was evicting because they had failed to honor Him as Lord. Because of their disobedience, He was giving the land to His people, Israel. The land would not be taken without some opposition. The Canaanites weren't going to give up their land without a fight. Walking into your destiny, claiming what God has for you, will not come without opposition. You will not get it without a fight. Too often the opposition we face is in the form of criticism from those closest to us, strategically shared to make you doubt what God promised you, whether or not you even deserve it, and if you have what it takes to get it. Don't allow yourself to be distracted or deterred by them.

They are like the folks I hung out with when I was growing up who said I would never go anywhere or be anything. The reality is they had no intentions of going anywhere and being anything themselves. Obviously, they saw something in my life that caused them to be envious.

Folks will try to stop you from stepping out of the rut you share with them. They don't want to see you get ahead of them and make something of yourself! Their criticisms are designed to cause doubt. Doubt will erode your confidence and cause you to be paralyzed by fear. Fear will keep you from moving forward and even cause you to give up on whatever it is you were going after.

You can't give up! This isn't just about you. If it is, then you have settled for worldly success that cannot promise fulfillment or an eternal reward. Your kingdom success is about what God wants to do through you for the benefit of others. God wants to strategically position you to transform the world. He wants to put you on display so that others, even your detractors, will see what happens to a man or woman who pursues his or her passion, giving them the confidence to pursue their own.

People are watching you; they know who you are and whose you are. They know who and what you represent! You are a son or daughter of the King! You were created to rule and reign with Him! You dare not hold back, intimidated by the opposition.

God has promised to take care of you. What can anyone do to you? God said, "No one will be able to stand up against you all the days of your life." He said through the prophet Isaiah 54:17, "No weapon formed against you will prevail, and you will refute every tongue that accuses you. This is the *heritage* of the servants of the Lord, and this is their vindication from me."

Paul, who constantly had people criticizing him, and accusing him in an effort to stop him from walking in his destiny, wrote to the saints in Rome: "If God is for us, who can be against us? He who did not spare his own Son, but gave Him up for us all —how will He not also, along with Him, graciously give us all things? Who will bring any charge against those whom God has chosen? It is God who justifies."

We are heirs of the promise; the chosen people of God! We were chosen to receive his unmerited favor. God knows all about us: the good, the bad, and the ugly we have done. He knows our strengths and our weaknesses, our gifts and our abilities. When He chose us and destined us for greatness, He knew what He was getting. We were chosen with divine intentionality by God, not for who we were then or even now, but what we will become in Him. We are on our way somewhere.

The third promise that God made is that of Eternal Presence. The reason God promised unending protection is that He was also making the promise of His unending presence. Verse 5 shows us this in God's Words, "As I was with Moses, so I will be with you; I will never leave you nor forsake you."

Whatever it is that God has called you to do is more than you can accomplish on your own. *God's assignments always require God's participation.* God has promised never to leave us or forsake us. Wherever He sends us; He goes with us, as a matter of fact, He is already there, preparing the way for us, opening doors, arranging meetings, strategic encounters to bless and provide for us whatever we need to succeed in that place.

Secured Possession, Unending Protection, and Eternal Presence are the promises that God himself makes to insure our success, but all these promises are conditional. We have to play our part. There are some things that God will not accomplish without our cooperation.

- God gives us the plan, but we have to work the plan.
- God promises us secured possessions, but we have to go after them.
- God promises unending protection, but we have to be courageous.

He told Joshua to be strong and very courageous! Being courageous is not the absence of fear, but the willingness to press on despite the presence of fear. God has promised us success, but we have to do those things that make success possible. The key element that God tells Joshua, as well as you and I in this passage, has to do with keeping His commandments and obeying His Word.

God made it clear to Joshua that if Israel was going to have success in taking the land, she would have to yield total obedience to the law of God. The Law of God was the written record where Moses kept all of God's Words and works, all of God's precepts and principles that He expected the people to obey, as a part of their covenant relationship with Him. It was imperative that they keep the commandments in the Promised Land, because they would constantly be tempted to follow the ways of the heathens living there and jeopardize God's blessing on their lives.

The same is true with us. We are so easily tempted to, while in Rome, do as the Romans do, forgetting that "though we are in the world, we are no longer of the world." We are citizens of a new kingdom that has its own values and standards recorded for us in our own book of the Law, the Bible.

If we are to be successful, God expects us to do just as He instructed Joshua and the people of Israel. We are to fully obey all the commands found in His Word and not turn to the right or to the left. Let me remind you that Israel did not fulfill their full destiny; they did not achieve the success that God had promised them because they never lived in complete obedience of the law.

I'm not quite sure what the problem was. Perhaps, they were like some of us who think that some of the commands of the Lord are unreasonable. Why would God expect us to live holy in an unholy world? Is there any joy in living holy? Aren't we supposed to be living the abundant life? Isn't the truth supposed to set us free? Why then should we have any restrictions imposed on us? We just need to be able to live free and do whatever we want.

I am sure that God would be cool with us living free if our nature was predisposed to living responsibly, but the truth of the matter is, every time we decide to do it our way and not His, we then have to call on Him to get us out of a mess we created.

God's idea of living free is freedom from bondage to our own passions and desires, freedom from the painful consequences of poor judgment and bad decisions, freedom from the guilt and shame that comes as a result of realizing that as hard as we try, the good that we would do is not what we do. But, that which we should not do is what we keep on doing.

God's idea of freedom is freedom to choose what is good, what is right, and what is best for us. This is the freedom we have in Christ. It is the Word of God that helps us live free! The Word of God is so awesome! There are so many benefits to obeying it, in addition to becoming successful and prosperous. Psalm 19 spells it out for us, beginning with verse seven.

The law of the Lord is perfect, flawless. It gives life to the soul, refreshing us and renewing us ,especially as we grow weary in the face of all the pressures and troubles of life.

The statutes of the law are trustworthy. We can depend on them to give us wisdom and understanding in an uncomplicated way when we are young, inexperienced, or just need guidance to make the right decision or the right choices in life.

The precepts of the Lord are right. They will never lead you wrong, but will produce joy in you from just knowing that you are living right—no guilt, no condemnation, and no shame.

The commands of the Lord are radiant, giving light to the eyes, light in darkness, clarity and understanding when we are confused and unable to find our way. The fear of the Lord is pure, enduring forever. The ordinances of the Lord are sure; they are steadfast; unchanging and independent of the circumstances of our lives.

We like to have the freedom to do what God says to do, or not to do, depending on the circumstances, as if morality, right and wrong are governed by circumstances. Right is right and wrong is wrong—no matter the situation. The Word of God is righteous and you will be righteous if you obey it!

When you have the Word in your heart, you are more confident and sure. You have a strong foundation upon which to stand. When you live by the Word, you don't have to second guess yourself and wonder if you are doing the right thing. When you know what you are supposed to do and you do it, there's an inner release; a sweet peace and joy that shows in everything you do, making you a cut above everyone else.

The Psalmist compares the Word to gold and honey. Gold refers to a larger and more prosperous life which you can have and expect more of, through the Word. Honey refers to satisfaction and fulfillment—the Word promises a life that is fulfilling and satisfying.

The Word keeps us on our toes because it constantly warns of the mistakes and pitfalls that can get us off track and cause us to miss out on what God has for us.

In keeping the law there is great reward. Have you noticed that attached to many of the precepts or commands of God, there is a promise of reward?

- Delight yourself in the Lord and He will give you the desires of your heart.
- Trust in the Lord with all your heart and lean not to your own understanding; in all your ways acknowledge Him and He will make your paths straight.
- Wait on the Lord, be of good courage and He will strengthen your heart.
- Give and it shall be given to you, good measure, pressed down, shaken together, and running over ...poured into your lap, for with the measure you use, it will be measured to you.
- Do not get weary in well doing, for in due season, you will reap if you faint not.

The way that Joshua would be sure to keep the law was that he was to never let it depart from his mouth. He was to meditate on it. The Hebrew word for meditate means *to mutter*. The Jews would often read the Word out loud or repeat it over and over again as they studied or reflected on the Word. As they continually spoke it to themselves, they were constantly thinking about it, being encouraged, comforted, convicted, and challenged by it. As they continually spoke it to themselves it was being written in their hearts and consciousness—transforming them.

It is not enough to think on the Word, we must be careful to do everything that it says. To do everything that it says is to not pick and choose. You know how we want to do what suits us, and then wonder why things don't fall into place? What God asks us to do is not optional. He has given us commands, not suggestions, for successful and prosperous living. And, He will not accept anything less than full obedience.

"Baggage Handlers"

A Sermon by MILLICENT HUNTER

Jeremiah 17:21 (King James Version)

"*Thus said the Lord; Take heed to yourselves, and bear no burden on the sabbath day; nor bring it in by the gates of Jerusalem.*"

Matthew 11: 28-30 (King James Version)

"*Come unto me, all ye that labour and are heavy laden, and I will give you rest. Take my yoke upon you, and learn of me; for I am meek and lowly in heart: and ye shall find rest unto your souls. For my yoke is easy and my burdened is light.*"

Exodus 20: 8-11 (King James Version)

"Remember the Sabbath day; to keep it holy. Six days shalt thou labour, and do all thy work: But the seventh day is the Sabbath of the Lord thy God: in it thou shall not do any work, thou, nor thy son, nor thou daughter, thy manservant, nor thy maidservant, nor thy cattle, nor thy stranger that is within thy gates. For in six days the Lord made heaven and earth, the sea, and all that in them is, and rested the seventh day: wherefore the Lord blessed the Sabbath day, and hallowed it."

There is something everyone over the age of five years old has in common. Can you guess what it is? It's not a physical characteristic like an eye, an arm, an ear or a leg, that's not where I'm going. But we all have one particular thing in common that makes us all a part of the human family and the human condition. Can you guess what that one thing might be?

This might shock you, but the answer is: we all have baggage. I'm not talking about baggage in the sense of a tangible item that you can touch, feel, pick up, manipulate and maneuver. No, not that is not the kind of baggage with which I'm referring. I'm talking about the baggage of experiences that we all have in our life. The kind of experiences that are brought on by the choices we make and the ways that we interact or respond to one another.

Baggage is a weight, it's a burden, and it's a load that we all carry. Either way, our baggage impacts our lives in very powerful ways, because it shapes us and molds our lives and influences the things we do and the decisions we make. Baggage contributes to who we are and how we live our lives in the world.

For the little ones, because they haven't had many experiences, their baggage is small. Their baggage is the size of a purse or a pocket book, a school bag or backpack. For others who have had a few more experiences in life, their baggage is like a carry-on because the load is heavy but it's manageable. Their load is cumbersome, but it can still be maneuvered and controlled. But for some of us, the issues and experiences that make up our baggage in life is so cumbersome and so burdensome and such a heavy load, that it's like a full set of psychological and spiritual luggage that we carry around in life. That's my assignment today; I want to talk about baggage handlers.

The longer you live, the more experiences you have, and the more experiences you have, the more you have to deal with. The more you have to deal with, the more you have to face. The more you have to face the more things you have to think about. The more things you have to think about, the more decisions you have to make. Each of the decisions you have to make, presents more opportunities to make the wrong decision, and that can be a weight, a burden, and a heavy load. These heavy loads can cause you to get up in the morning wondering what the day is going to bring that could turn out to be a weight, that could be a burden, that could be a heavy load, that could be baggage.

If you don't know what to do about the weight, if you don't know how to handle the heavy load, if you don't know what to do with the burden, if you don't know how to handle the baggage, then pretty soon you'll suffer from stress attacks and anxiety attacks, high blood pressure, hypertension nervous break downs, personality disorders and mood swings. You'll find yourself yelling and snapping at people, fighting and cussing people out. People will not understand what's wrong with you. It's all because you're handling baggage. You're dealing with issues and stresses and the heavy loads of life. As soon as you get tired of all of that mess being on your back here comes something else. And if you go to someone for help, you'll find that they are not equipped to help you because they have a full time job trying to help him/herself.

Baggage is unavoidable. It's something that everyone starts accumulating early in life. It is something that even little children have. You give birth to them and they look so cute and innocent, so fresh and new. You dress them up, put baby oil and baby powder on them and outfit them with cute clothes and they look adorable. You try to protect them as much as you can. However, I don't care if you keep them locked up in a safe environment, away from all predators and abusers and negative influences that come with living, you still cannot protect them from baggage. You cannot keep them from accumulating the weight and heavy load of just living from day to day, because it is inherent in human nature that ultimately life brings baggage.

That is why so many marriages end in divorce. We marry, hoping to find someone who will take the weight off of us, and as soon as we get to know him or her we find out that they have baggage too. The combination of your mess and their mess becomes so heavy that the marriage gets weak. The marriage begins to break because the woman wasn't looking for a man, the woman was looking for a messiah. The man wasn't looking for a wife, the man was looking for a maid. The man was looking for someone to clean up his mess—fix his life and make him feel better about himself. But the reality is that whoever you marry, also has baggage. Keep in mind, they're just as messed up as you are.

As soon as you find out their secrets you start saying things like, "Maybe I married the wrong person", "or he/she's not the one for me", or "I'm falling out of love". No, that's not it; it's just a combination of your bags and his/her bags that are so heavy that the ship begins to sink. Ladies, I don't care how fine he is, don't let him fool you. He may be 6'4" and fine. He may be good-looking, have six-pack abs and every other kind of pack, but beneath that hairy chest and those big biceps, brother got some baggage.

He is damaged goods. His cologne barely covers up the stench of a lifetime of watching his father abuse his mother. He is damaged goods from the weight of watching his father treat his mother with disrespect. He carries the heavy load of never seeing what a healthy marriage looks like because all he ever saw was other men walking out on their wives and abandoning their children. He is damaged goods because he carries the weight of watching people deal with stress by drinking, drugging and running away from any situation that was a challenge.

As hard as he tries to get up in the morning and say, "I am not going to be like that" he picks up the same baggage and ends up doing the same thing to someone else and repeats the pattern. And brothers, believe me when I tell you that sister might look like a Coca-Cola bottle, 36"-24"-36", but while you're adding up those numbers, add in the weight of her past. Add in the weight of her childhood and the life she had before you came along, because while you're carrying her over the threshold, it's not just her you're carrying, she has baggage.

You're carrying her momma, and her grand momma, and her great grand momma and all the things that happened to them at the hands of the men in their lives. You're carrying the weight of what her first boyfriend did to her, how he broke her heart, and then the man who dumped her and her first baby daddy who walked out on her. Her baggage includes the dude who violated her, betrayed her, disappointed her and abused her. You're carrying that weight over the threshold when you pick up sister girlfriend. We are all baggage handlers!

What does all of that handling of baggage do to us? For the believer, Sunday is our Sabbath. Sunday is our day of rest; it is supposed to be a day that we set aside for worship. Sabbath is supposed to be the day that we cease from all our labors. Sabbath, this is supposed to be the believer's "chill time" if you will. Tell your neighbor, "I'm just chillin'". We're supposed to come aside and fellowship together with our church family. This is a time when we're supposed to come together to worship God for who God is and to look back on our week and praise God for all that God done for us.

Sabbath is the one time in the week, one day out of seven, where we're supposed to gather together to hear the Word preached and to join in and enjoy the singing of the songs of Zion. But the baggage that some of you are handling causes you to stay home on Sundays or go other places and do other things. The baggage that you're handling, causes you to take on a second and third job on Sunday, and then work yourself in the ground. You have another job during the week but the baggage you're handling causes you to chase money, so much so that you sweat and toil and burn the candle at both ends.

You have to rob Peter to pay Paul, because you're making money, but you feel like you have a hole in your pocket because you can't hold on to your money. Or you make it here, but you bring your issues to the house of God. You don't leave your baggage at home, you bring it right up in here with you, every weight and every burden that you have and sit it in the seat next to you. You bring the heavy load of the baggage of your issues and circumstances and place it at your feet so that you can't move and the people around you can't move either.

When you're handling so much baggage it closes your mind so that you hear the Word, but you don't apply it. You see everyone else around you praising the Lord, but you're stuck in a rut. You're so beat down by the heavy load of everything that you're carrying that the area around you is crammed tight with spiritual and psychological luggage. You can't budge, you can't say amen, you can't say hallelujah all you can do is sit there and stare straight ahead because you're handling so much baggage. Ask your neighbor, "*Can you move your luggage out of my way, please? Thank you. Come on, move that suitcase, get that baggage out of here."*

That's what happened in our text. I took the time to read Jeremiah because Jeremiah brings up an issue about the Sabbath that I would like to talk about with you for a few moments. Jeremiah says that the Lord says, "Take heed to yourselves" and bear no burden on the Sabbath day nor bring it in by the gates of Jerusalem, neither carry forth the burden out of your house neither do ye any work, but keep the Sabbath day holy as I commanded your fathers then the Lord says, "The people didn't obey, they didn't even listen but they made their necks stiff so that they could not hear and as a result God allowed judgment to come against his people."

In other words, the Lord is saying to us, "I don't want to see you coming into my presence, overwhelmed and all bogged down with stuff "that hinders your praise and stifles your worship and gets in the way of a real experience with me". The Lord says don't even bring that stuff out of your house, into My house because I don't want to see you up under a load on the Sabbath day. Don't bring your issues, don't bring your burdens, and don't bring your situations and circumstances. The Lord says in the Old Testament don't bring that stuff to My house on the Sabbath.

What is the Sabbath? One of the signs of the covenant that God made with Israel in the Old Testament was the Sabbath day. I can remember when one of my Sunday school teachers took me to the New Testament and showed me a scripture in the book of Acts that said on the first day of the week they came together and she did that to help me understand the New Testament Sabbath is on Sunday and that it was the New Testament Sabbath because it represented a new beginning.

Christ rose from the dead on the 3rd day, which was the 1st day of the week, and so from the New Testament forward we should worship on Sunday. And while I respect that theology and reasoning, I don't want to make a doctrine out of it because I think there is a deeper revelation. I grew up in the Baptist Church and in the Baptist Church, back in the day, we went to Sunday school and Vacation Bible school and they taught us about the Sabbath day. There was a great debate going on at that time as to what day was the real day to worship God. The debate continues.

In spite of the fact that the New Testament tells us to not be a respecter of days, some folks are still debating over what day we ought to worship. I have some good friends who are Sabbath Keepers and Seventh-day Adventists who worship the Lord on Saturdays. According to the Hebrew calendar, Saturday is the Sabbath day. I have absolutely no problem with anyone who chooses to go to church on Saturday I have no problem with that. I would never debate that, I would never argue about that. I can pass by the Sabbath Keepers Church or the Seventh-Day Adventist church, and wave —respect and appreciate their right to worship God on Saturday because I worship God on Saturday too, yeah, I do!

Now I hope that that does not exempt me from the opportunity to serve as a pastor. I hope that no one calls any meetings on me at the church. I hope that the key still fits the door in my office when I come to preach next Sunday. But I do worship on Saturday; as a matter of fact ever since I've been saved I've worshiped on Saturday, and Friday, and Thursday, and Wednesday, and generally on Tuesday, and Monday. I worship on Sunday also, because I don't have to come to a building to be in worship. It doesn't have to be any particular day of the week for me to be in worship. I worship the Lord wherever I am and wherever I go. The Sabbath was made for man; man was not made for the Sabbath.

The Sabbath represents rest and peace unto the Lord. Now understand this, I don't want to get real heavy but I want to give you a little bit of Bible class so that you can appreciate where I'm going. The Old Testament teaches us, in the form of a shadow, what God has in mind. The New Testament reveals the Old Testament shadow, as the New Testament reality. In the Old Testament, God teaches us about rest by showing us a day. A day, an "eon" is representative of an age. God wants us to understand that there is a period and a time where a man is to enter into rest. You will minimize the plan of God if you diminish this period down to a 24-hour period. In the shadow of the Old Testament, it may be a 24-hour period but in the reality of the New Testament, it is the day of grace in which we live right now. Now what caused God the Father in creation to bring us into rest is that He had finished from His labor and announced that He was finished by entering into His rest.

And when Christ died, he said tele - telesti' which in Aramaic means it is finished. He then hung his head in the locks of his shoulders on Calvary's cross and finished the work of redemption. So what God the Father did in the Old Testament at the end of the creation by entering into the rest, God the Son did in redemption when he ceased from his labor of redemption. And when Jesus said, "It is finished", it echoed all the way back to the Old Testament when the Father had finished His creation. And when the Lord had finished His redemptive process, the Bible says that your Lord and my God sat down on the right hand of the Majesty of God and entered into His rest. This is the rest that the Lord wants the church to come into not a 24-hour period, not the memory of the day. You will find that the keeping of a day of rest is a covenant between God and the nation of Israel, but the book of Hebrews says that God has provided some better thing for us. It is appropriate that the Jews should keep the Sabbath day because the Jews are still waiting on the Messiah to come, but it is ridiculous for the church to walk away with the shadow when we have the bridegroom.

Ten years ago at 2 o'clock in the afternoon on June 26 at our former location in Philadelphia, Pennsylvania, my husband and I got married. We stood in front of the preacher, Bishop Vashti McKenzie. Like any good light, the beautiful sunshine of a June afternoon was casting colorful shadows through the stained-glass windows on the walls of the sanctuary. There were bridesmaids and bridegrooms all around and ribbons and flowers everywhere. I stood at the back of the church and floated down the aisle on air. I don't even remember walking down the aisle; I just floated. As Bishop McKenzie pronounced us husband and wife, I didn't walk away with a shadow, I walked away with the man.

It seems ridiculous for the New Testament church to be espoused unto Jesus Christ and walk away holding on to the shadow when we can walk away holding on to Jesus Christ himself. The book of Hebrews says that God has provided something better for us. Hebrews 4 says, *"let us labor to enter into that rest"*. All through the Old Testament God taught us to fight our way into that rest. That's why the Levitical priests were forbidden to work outside the temple like the other tribes. When they entered into the temple, they entered into the rest of the Lord. The Old Testament teaches that there should be no sweat in the Holy of Holies, do whatever you have to do to get into that rest.

There is a rest that Christ offers to the church that is so powerful and so important that if you ever enter into that rest, you will literally not worry about a thing. God is trying to tell you that there is a place in Him where there is no sweat at all, where you can rest in the Lord. You will notice in your walk with God that once you get into a certain dimension of faith things that used to bother you doesn't bother you anymore. Things that should upset you don't upset you anymore because you have entered into the rest of the Lord. What you have to do is fight away anyone who would pull you - out of the rest. Touch someone and say, now that I'm asleep, don't wake me up. Now that I've finally stopped trying to save myself, fix myself, deliver myself, pull myself out, don't wake me up with your doubt, your fear, your unbelief, your negative stinkin' thinkin' and attitude. It took me half of my life to finally enter into this rest and I'm not going to let anyone pull me back out of the rest.

We sing a familiar stanza from Psalm 119—
*This is the day that the Lord hath made, we shall
rejoice and be glad in it.* That's a great song to sing
but we are not the first ones to sing it, Israel has been
singing it for years and years and years, It was a part of
the process of the Passover in fact, you will remember
in the New Testament that when Christ had finished
saying take eat, this is my body that was broken for
you and after the same manner, he lifted up the cup
and they all drank together and the Bible says that
they sang a hymn and they went out into the Mount
of Olives. Now, I don't know the tune of that hymn
but the words of the hymn was, *This is the day that
the Lord hath made we shall rejoice and be glad in
it.* They're not talking about a 24 hour period they're
talking about a day of atonement. They're talking
about a day where a man is not judged by works, not
by labor, not by sweat, but he's entered into the grace
of God and ceased from his labor. When Jesus had
them sing that song and they went away singing that
song, it was because he had ushered in a new day.
Touch someone and say this is a new day.

This is the good news that Jesus said the Spirit of
the Lord God hath anointed me to preach the gospel.
This is the good news that they've been waiting to
hear that we are not saved by works lest any man
should boast. This is the good news that salvation
is the gift of God, freely given to those who will
receive that grace. This is the grace that made Jesus
cry out. There are two times in the New Testament
when Jesus screamed. One Greek word he screamed
out before God was "crut zo". And another Greek
word he screamed out was "Ho", this was when he
cried out, "Let every man that thirst come unto me".

The good news is, the Word of the Lord gives us a solution to all of this. Christ is standing there saying, *"Come unto me all of you that are weak and heavy laden and I will give you rest, take my yoke upon you and learn of me for my yoke is easy and my burden is light"*. Most of you shout about it, and some of you dance about, it but you've never responded to it and entered into the rest of the Lord.

This is the first general invitation from Christ expressed in the Bible. In order to make this journey successfully, you have to make it without baggage. You can't carry loads of baggage and weight on you. In order to be free, Jesus gives you an invitation to come unto him and you have to come unto him because you will not receive rest from anyone else. I think one of the most important things that our faith offers to us today is a resting place. A resting place doesn't begin in the New Testament but refers back to the Old Testament. I so deeply appreciate the way David brags about God's resting place in the 23rd Psalm. David says, "The Lord is my shepherd I shall not want he maketh me to lie down in green pastures, he leadeth me beside the still waters he restoreth my soul". The still waters: is a place of rest where we can drink and slake our thirst and find green grass. Not because of our own strength and ingenuity, but because of the relationship that we have with the Shepherd himself. The Psalmist describes us as sheep who are dependent, in need of leadership and guidance. This description is not to insult our intelligence but to explain the vulnerability that we have between us and God. By comparison, all of our wisdom is foolishness in the mind of God, and when we find ourselves engaged in conflict that is overwhelming, if God doesn't make a way for us, we will never get out on our own. Say that with me, I will never get out on my own.

You'd be surprised at how long you can live not knowing that you cannot get yourself out of anything by yourself. You can't find anyone who can get you out and will eventually you will come to a point where you recognize that you'll never get out on your own. Then you begin to realize that other people can't get you out of a tight spot either. You can go to someone else for help and find out that they have as many, possibly more problems than you. If you're broke, they're lame...if you're distraught, they're depressed...if you're full of fear, they're desperate. Sooner or later, you will recognize that each of us carries something that only God can lift off of us. Ultimately, you find yourself in a place where you significantly need the Lord in your life in a powerful way. The Lord says to you, "I scream when I see you thirsting for things that I already have to give you. Why are you worried about stuff that I've already taken care of? Why are you burdened about things that I've already moved out of the way? Come unto me all that are weak and heavy laden and I will give you rest."

I'm going to give you three pieces of baggage that you need to get rid of if you're going to make this journey. There is the baggage of sin we each are born with it. Scripture says we are shaped in iniquity. This sin existed in us before we ever acted on it or earned it. Sin is inherent in our nature.

I was born into the state of sin before I ever committed an act of sin. It is a weight that messes up my peace. It destroys my joy; it causes me to be discontent in situations I ought to be content in. It frustrates me in secret places, it's a bag you cannot see, it's my cargo, the baggage of sin.

Past sin is the second bag. Now notice that there is a distinction between sin and past sins. Sin is a state and sins are an act. Christ didn't just come to deliver me from my sins (s - i - n - s) Christ came to deliver me from my sin, the state of sin. Christ came to deliver me from the act of sin. Not delivering me from the state of sin is like cutting the fruit off the tree and leaving the root there. I have to deal with the state of sin and I have to deal with the act of sin. Here lies the challenge—I can't do anything about the state of sin, Christ has got to deal with that. One of the things the enemy does, even to those who are saved, is that he keeps you aware of the acts of sin, your past sins. That's why we baptize you. It places a line of demarcation between you and your past sins. Through baptism, you bury your past sins, eradicating them, drawing a line in the sand and saying that old man is dead—he is no longer alive anymore. Baptism is saying, I rise up to walk in the newness of life. Yet many of us have not taken advantage, because you're still wrestling with stuff that's over, past sins.

Some of us are struggling with present sins, issues that are confronting us now - secret sins, secret issues, that break up our fellowship, destroy our peace stop us from being happy, stop us from enjoying our lives. You're all dressed up, but you're still carrying baggage, sin. Sin, it's a baggage, it's a weight. Every weakness is a weight. Every strange, illicit conversation, every wandering through the worldwide web in the middle of the night — is a weight.

The baggage of sin disrupts marriages, destroys homes, and disrupts peace. The baggage of sin, just one act, action or reaction, can land a good person locked up in jail, the baggage of sin. There's not one person that hasn't been smeared with it. No one in this world can outrun it—from the educated to the illiterate, Anglos and Africans, Hispanics, Asians— ethnicity makes no difference. Everyone has baggage smeared with sin. People in tribes in the deepest part of Africa, kings and princes in palaces, royal families and poor families, are all exposed to the baggage of sin.

You can sit there all dressed up, hair clean, smelling like deodorant and real expensive cologne— but in order to make this journey, you have to make it without baggage. In order to be free, you can't carry loads of baggage. Jesus gives you an open invitation to come unto Him. Come unto Him because you cannot receive rest from anyone else. In the words of a sacred hymn, "What can wash away my sins? Nothing but the blood of Jesus. What can make me whole again, nothing but the blood of Jesus!"

" *It's Just a Test* "

A Sermon by SHARMA D. LEWIS

James 1: 2-3 (New King James Version)

" **M** y brethren, count it all joy when you fall
into various trials, knowing that the testing
of your faith, produces patience. "

Rick Warren, author of *The Purpose Driven Life*,
believes that God views life as a test, a trust, and
a temporary assignment.[1] As we read the Bible, we
see this point validated throughout the scriptures.
Warren further explains how God continuously tests
our character, faith, obedience, love, integrity, and
loyalty.[2] Words like trials, temptations, refining, and
testing occur more than 200 times in the Bible.[3]
Do you sometimes feel that life is just a test? Over

the course of this past year, did you feel that you've been tested in nearly every aspect of your life? Did you convince yourself that this year was going to be better that the ones before, but soon noticed Satan has increased the warfare against your life?

God tested Adam and Eve to see if they could remain obedient to a straightforward request. God tested Abraham by asking him to offer his son Isaac as a burnt offering. God tested Moses to see if he would accept the assignment to help direct the Israelites out of Egypt. God tested Joshua to see if he would lead his people into the Promise Land. God tested Gideon to see if he would trust God and downsize his army. God tested Hannah when God closed, and then opened, her womb. God tested Esther to take a stance for her people. God tested Job faithfulness when he lost all of his possessions. God tested Jeremiah when God called him, in his young age, to be a prophet. God tested the three Hebrew boys to see if they would bow down to Nebuchadnezzar. God tested Paul with the constant reminder of the thorn in his flesh. You may be presently under the microscope of one life's many tests.

God tests you when it's time to get to church. Satan tries to stop you by pulling out all types of distractions. The phone rings, the kids aren't ready, your spouse starts acting funny, you discover a run in your stockings (and that was your last pair!), and you already woke up debating whether or not you were going to Church.

God is testing you with your finances. In this economy, will you be faithful in giving your tithes and offerings? Will you be content with the blessings of God? Or, will you live above your means: buying clothes, buying cars, going on trips you can't afford, and buying houses to impress your neighbors, while rarely, if ever, acknowledging God.

God tests marriages. He tests you — as you stood before your pastor, your family, and your friends. You recited your vows, "for better, for worse, for richer, for poorer, in sickness and in health, to love and to cherish, until we are parted by death; this is my solemn vow."[4] How many of you can agree, that, as soon as you said "I do," you were presented with a test?

God is testing clergymen and women. Do we *Service* yearn for our colleagues' ministries, because, on the outside looking in, what they have looks glamorous? Are we faithful; or is it just we desire to be famous? Do we give God our best; or do we give Him our leftovers and sloppy seconds? Do we live a life of holiness; or do we duck and dodge, thinking that God won't hold us accountable? Do we preach warm, fuzzy, intellectual sermons to keep our parishioners content and happy in their sins; or do we preach the bold, unadulterated truth, which empowers, enlightens, and equips our parishioners to be better Christians? Do we hear from God concerning the people who are hurting and suffering in our churches?

Several years ago, God put me through a test in my ministry. In the United Methodist Church, we are appointed and re-appointed each year to a church. In 2004, I was appointed to a predominantly Euro-congregation with an average age of sixty-five. History was being made at this church! I was the first woman to be appointed to this church in fifty years, and the very first Black. The church had struggled for many years in several areas.

Prior to being appointed to the new church, I served the Senior Associate Pastor of Christian Training at a predominantly Black congregation. This congregation was vibrant, growing, loving, and affirming to a single Black female, new in the ministry. Unfortunately, my new assignment was quite difficult and I found myself praying relentlessly to God. I prayed so much that I could count the "carpet fibers" next to my bed. Several members left the church and withheld their financial giving because of my appointment. I remember one woman sharing with me that she couldn't follow my vision and she then left the church. My response to her was, "Do not follow my vision, follow God's vision."

Beloved, I don't know the test that God will send down your path; but my momma and daddy would often say that if you "just keep living," you will be tested in your life. I agree with Rick Warren, we don't know all the tests God will give us, but we can predict some of them, based on His Word. You will be tested by major changes, delayed promises, impossible problems, unanswered prayers, undeserved criticism, and even senseless tragedies.[5]

Let us examine the text found in James 1:2-3, *"my brethren count it all joy, when you fall into various trials, knowing that the testing of your faith produces patience"* (NKJV). As we examine the text, major theological issues wrestle with faith and works. James is an eclectic letter filled with moral advice, piercing wisdom, practical instruction, and socioeconomic commentary.[6] James opens this epistle by sharing how to understand trials and tribulations as an opportunity to grow in our faith. He then goes on to shows the reader how to love God during these trials and tribulations, and reveals what qualities are needed for enduring the trials.

James, who considers himself a slave of God and of the Lord Jesus Christ, is challenging his brothers and sisters to face their trials with a sense of joy.[7] He claims that the testing of one's faith, resulting from trials, produces spiritual discipline *(hypomone)*.[8] *Hypomone,* generally translated as patience or endurance, has been interpreted quite convincingly as "militant patience" or "nonviolent resistance."[9] James is calling for spiritual discipline that will provide strength, support, and a connection to God in the face of various hardships.[10]

The African American mystic, theologian, and pastor, Howard Thurman, the grandson of a slave, knew about such spiritual discipline.[11] In his book, *Disciplines of the Spirit,* Thurman discussed ways in which commitment, wisdom, suffering, prayer, and reconciliation can be cultivated as spiritual resources for overcoming trials.[12]

Beloved, please allow me to give you three insights so that you may make it through a test. The first insight is: during a test, you must understand that God is shaping your character. Webster's New Collegiate Dictionary defines character as, "the group of qualities that makes a person."[13] I agree with Rick Warren, that character is both developed and revealed by a test. God uses situations to develop our character. Warren states that God depends more on circumstances to make us more like Jesus than he depends on us reading the Bible. This is because, as believers, we will face circumstances, trials, and tribulations 24 hours a day. I believe that our character is being constantly molded everyday of our lives.

I remember growing up in Statesboro, Georgia, and when I faced obstacles, I could hear my mother's voice repeating these words, "Sharma, through trials and hard times God is testing and shaping your character." She would always remind me that "no one comes into this world pain free" and "life is full of test and trials." Character building is a slow process. Whenever we try to avoid or escape the problems of life, we short-circuit the process, delaying our Christian growth and stunting our spiritual maturity. I believe that every test we encounter is a character building opportunity. My mother would always reassure me that I could make it. She would repeat, in her firm and loving tone, "you are made of good Lewis stock."

This comment triggered another thought: as believers we are made out of good stock. We are made in the image of God. You must remember that God made you with God-self in mind. We are made out of prime stock. My Bible reveals that we are "fearfully and wonderfully made" (Psalm 139:14, NKJV). We are made from the stock that has benefits. We have medical insurance: God's Word states, *"and by His stripes we are healed"* (Isaiah 53:5, NKJV). We have life insurance: God's Word states, *"if you believe in Him you will have everlasting life"* (John 3:16, NKJV). We have a 100 percent deductible: Jesus Christ paid it all on Calvary.

On this Christian journey, passing life's tests show how we've overcome the obstacles that confront us. Tests and trials are outward circumstances encountered by all believers. In the text, believers are to consider trials as opportunities for rejoicing. I believe that the trials we face and the character building we endure are not only for our growth, but they serve as a testimony for others in our lives. God's Word reveals that the "father knowest" (Matthew 6:8, KJV). God knows who He can trust with certain trials and obstacles. For example, God knows that some of us can't yet handle marriage. Marriage was ordained as a covenant by God. Covenants are binding. When problems appear in marriage, instead of seeking God to fight to protect the covenant, a person unprepared for the challenge would run.

Troubles and difficulties are tools used in the testing, refining, and purifying of our faith. They are tools which assist in producing the characteristics of patience and endurance. The aim of testing is not to destroy you or to afflict you, but to purge and refine you. First Peter 1:7 states that *"the test we endure brings praise, honor, and glory at the revelation of Jesus Christ"* (NKJV).

The second insight of making it through a test is that you must cast your burden onto the Lord. There is a familiar song written by Isaac Balinda, entitled *"Cast your burdens unto Jesus, for He cares for you."*[14] First Peter 5:7 states, *"casting all your care upon Him, for He cares for you"* (NKJV). To "cast" means to give it up. God wants me to encourage you to stop fighting the obstacles and give them up to Him.

The psalmist reveals in Psalm 55:22, *"to cast your burden on the Lord and He shall sustain you; He shall never permit the righteous to be moved"* (NKJV). To "sustain you" means to give support or relief. To "sustain you" means to supply you with nourishment.

As Christians we must recognized that the Lord is the one constant in our lives. Jobs and people change everyday. Jesus Christ can bear the burden, because Jesus is our "burden bearer." He was spit on, ridiculed, hung high, and stretched wide. Why do we think that, in the midst of our trials and tests, Jesus wouldn't be able to handle our burdens? God's Word instructs, in Matthew 11:28-30, *"come to Me, all you who labor and are heavy laden, and I will give you rest. Take My yoke upon you and learn from Me, for I am gentle and lowly in heart, and you will find rest for your soul. For My yoke is easy and My burden is light"* (NKJV).

Finally, the third insight in making it through a test is to keep Jesus Christ at the center of the crisis. When things happen in our lives, our first human instinct is to take control. We think we can intellectualize God. We think we can handle our own problems, without God.

If we reflect and examine our African American culture, I think you would understand when I say, that to make it through a test, we must keep Christ at the center of the crisis. If Christ was not at the center during slavery, how did mothers cope when their husbands were whipped and lynched, their children were taken away, and they were repeatedly raped by their slave masters? If Christ was not at the center, how did some of you make it in the 60s, when many Black Americans experienced harsh segregation? Single parents, if Christ was not at the center, how did you cope when "baby daddy," or "baby momma," was not around to help with the children? If not but for Christ, how did you make it when the absent parent did not come through on paying the bills?

The text reminds us that the testing of our faith produces patience or endurance in life. God wants us to pass the test of life. God will never allow you to face a test that is greater than the grace that He has already given you to handle them. The Bible says, *"God keeps his promise, and He will not allow you to be tested beyond your power to remain firm; at the time you are put to a test, He will give you the strength to endure it and will provide you with a way out of it"* (1 Corinthians 10:13, TEV). Every time you pass a test, God rewards you in heaven. The Bible reveals, *"blessed is the man who perseveres under trial, because when he has stood the test, he will receive the crown of life that God has promised to those who love him"* (James 1:12, NIV).

[handwritten: Promise Keeper]

Problems force us to depend on God instead of ourselves. My belief is that you'll never truly know that God is all you need until God is all you have. A Christian is like a tea bag, not much good until it has gone through some hot water.[15] As Christians, we must come to understand that God uses problems to draw us closer to His Word. The Bible states that *"the Lord is close to the brokenhearted and saves those who are crushed in spirit"* (Psalm 34:18, NIV).

Beloved, allow me to encourage you to keep Christ at the center of your crisis. None of our problems could happen without God's permission. We have the assurance, as Christians, that *"all things work together for good to those who love God, to those who are the called according to His purpose"* (Romans 8:28, NJKV).   So, remember, when life has thrown you a curve, it's just a test. When your relationship is not progressing, it's just a test. When you are criticized, it's just a test. When you are rejected, it's just a test. When you are persecuted, it's just a test. When you've been struck by an unexpected illness, it's just a test. When prayers haven't been answered, it's just a test. When your marriage is on shaky ground, it's just a test. When you've been laid off, it's just a test. Amen.

"When You Are In Over Your Head"

A sermon by SUSIE C. OWENS

Genesis 22:1-5; 8-18 (King James Version)

*A nd it came to pass, after these things, God did
tempt Abraham, and said unto him, Abraham:
and he said, Behold, here I am. And he said, Take
now thy son, thine only son Isaac, whom thou lovest,
and thee unto the land of Moriah; and offer him there
for a burnt offering upon one of the mountains I will tell
thee of. And Abraham rose up early in the morning, and
saddled his ass, and took two of his young men with
him, and Isaac his son, and clave the wood for the burnt
offering, and rose up, and went unto the place of which
God had told him. Then on he third day Abraham lifted
up his eyes and saw the place afar off. And Abraham said
unto the young men, Abide ye here with the ass; and I*

and the lad will go yonder and worship, and come again unto you. And Abraham said, My son, God will provide himself a lamb for a burnt offering: so they went both of them together. And they came to the place which God had told him of; and Abraham built an altar there, and laid the wood in order, and bound Isaac his son, and laid him on the altar upon the wood. And Abraham stretched forth his hand, and took the knife to slay his son. And the angel of the LORD called unto him out of heaven, and said, Abraham, Abraham: and he said, Here am I. And he said, Lay not thine hand upon the lad, neither do thou any thing unto him: for now I know that thou fearest God, seeing thou hast not withheld thy son, thine only son from me. And Abraham lifted up his eyes, and looked, and behold behind him a ram caught in a thicket by his horns: and Abraham went and took the ram, and offered him up for a burnt offering in the stead of his son. And Abraham called the name of that place Jehovah-jireh: as it is said to this day, In the mount of the LORD it shall be seen. And the angel of the LORD called unto Abraham out of heaven the second time, And said, By myself have I sworn, saith the LORD, for because thou hast done this thing, and hast not withheld thy son, thine only son: That in blessing I will bless thee, and in multiplying I will multiply thy seed as the stars of the heaven, and as the sand which is upon the sea shore; and thy seed shall possess the gate of his enemies; And in thy seed shall all the nations of the earth be blessed; because thou hast obeyed my voice.

The phrase "in over your head" is part of a group of idioms that have found their way into African American colloquialism. Although they may not be perfect English, they make perfect sense. I'm sure you are familiar with many of them. Some are the expressions you've heard Mama and Grandma say things like: "everything that glitters ain't gold"; "don't judge a book by its cover"; "what you see ain't always what you get"; and the very popular one, "the grass always looks greener on the other side of the fence." When one is in over one's head, the suggestion is that you are in a difficult situation that is beyond your understanding, beyond your brain power, or area of expertise.

Perhaps, Abraham would have found refuge in those statements. Maybe it would have provided some consultation for those thoughts to be present when God made the request for Abraham to give the life of his son as an offering. Before we examine the text closer, let's examine why God would ask something like this from Abraham in the first place. Why would God consider, even remotely, that Abraham would do such a drastic thing? Two trains of thought come to mind: Abraham's faith and Abraham's obedience.

For a moment, let's deal with Abraham's faith, which, as one would expect, was a collage of ups and downs. The ups and downs were incurred from the numerous trials and tests that he faced over his lifetime, which worked him in ways that expanded his ability to trust in God. You must always keep in mind, a believer's walk with God is a walk of faith. Faith can only be matured through the endurance of stressful trials, tribulations, and persecutions. Faith *comes* by hearing the message of Christ (Romans 10:17), but the developing and maturing process is reserved for hands-on training.

Faith also requires that works are performed alongside it. James reminds us that faith without works is dead. Our works must be a testimony of what we believe, and what we believe must coincide with what we do. Abraham's faith building journey with God began when God requested that he leave his familiar surroundings and follow God's instructions. Those instructions brought him into a new dwelling place, where his faith development began. Imagine how difficult it must have been to leave the comfort of the familiar. Then, God raised the stakes, and requested the unthinkable... kill Isaac!

Kill Isaac? Kill the son of promise! Kill the seed, through who nations are supposed to be born? What possible good could emerge from this? When life presents you with this kind of question, keep in mind that strong faith is often developed in the tensions of life's challenges. Faith demonstrates itself more fully in the hard places of life. Here, God is stretching Abraham's parental love to the maximum, and he's doing it on a stage of faith. It was on this same stage, a few years earlier, that Abraham, in his old age, had to believe God for Isaac's birth. One must wonder how God really evaluates our faith. What is clear, even if the evaluation process is cloudy, is, without faith, it is impossible to please God.

Secondly, let's examine Abraham's walk of obedience, which was an extreme one! What kind of man, who was blessed to father a son in the twilight years of his life, would be willing to take the life of that child, on God's command? The task that is set before Abraham is one that will allow God to demonstrate how obedience is better than sacrifice. Man's call to obedience must be attached to his performance.

God had faith in Abraham's ability to trust His wisdom. So, God knew He could count on Abraham's ability to obey Him, regardless of the circumstance. Likewise, Abraham had confidence in God's ability to carry out His promises. Abraham must have had some encounters with God that suggested to him, God would never ask anything of him that ultimately wouldn't turn out for his good.

We are expected to live a life of faith, and our faith must progress. Last year's faith can only serve as a catalyst for this year's growth and further faith development. God never tests us in areas that He has not previously prepared us for. Consequently, there had to have been some prior faith encounters to solidify this unusual request from God.

How you grow in God or how you have grown in God has very little to do with materialistic gain, but has everything to do with how well you can handle the tests and trials that come your way. Therefore, material prosperity, at any moment in one's life, cannot be the measuring rod by which we measure one's faith. The ability to keep the faith through the struggles should be a benchmark for faithful servants.

Abraham is asked by God to take Isaac and offer him as a Burnt offering unto the Lord. The Burnt offering was unlike the Peace offering, the Absolution offering, or the Compensation offering, where only certain animal body parts were removed. Unlike these offerings, the Burnt offering required the total consumption of the animal. It represented the total submission and dedication of one's self to God becoming a sweet aroma to Him.

From the onset of the request, Abraham knew that Isaac's life was on the line. He was not oblivious to the requirements related to the sacrifice. The lesson for us to remember is that faith requires you to place your entire self on the line if God's purposes are to be fulfilled in your life. Keep in mind that, obedience is better than sacrifice. Let me further suggest that a believer usually gets to a place where it is "over their head" when complying with some extraordinary command from God. If we never reached that point, when would we need faith?

Let's bring it home. Commands of faith will require us to make personal sacrifices, such as cutting off a relationship when you so enjoy that person's company; giving an extra one hundred dollars in the offering this week when you have already earmarked that money for something else; or getting up at 5:00 am over the next six weeks to pray (God knows you are not a morning person). God's faith building requests often remove us from our comfort zone. Such was the case and point of the text. Abraham takes Isaac and begins to prepare him to be the sacrifice. He shows us that you must be unwavering in your commitment to the process and your obedience to the request, no matter how outlandish it seems.

Setting himself to obey God's request, meant stepping out on what he already knew of God—embracing a new leg of the journey, which then led to a level of trust that had not previously been breached. Abraham may not have expected that the breaching of this new area was designed to bring him into a wealthy place, built with faith. He was already "in over his head" because of his covenant relationship with God, which branded him as a faith walker. He's already accustomed to trusting God, in spite of what it looks like. As they journeyed, Isaac asked, "Where are we going?" Abraham's response, "we are going to worship."

Three observations are made in studying this text. The first is, when you are "in over your head," be sure not to neglect worship. You must strive to keep an attitude of worship... count it all joy! When what you are dealing with doesn't make any sense, just give God thanks and praise, because you know He hasn't left you. The Bible states, "In everything, give thanks, for this is the will of God concerning you" (1 Thessalonians 5:18). Knowing that, God inhabits the praises of His people, and in His presence there is fullness of joy, at his right hand pleasures forevermore; finding something to thank and praise Him for should be easy. When you worship God in a hard spot, you are saying to God, "no matter what I'm going through, serving You is worth it!" This is when your praise and worship become weapons against the enemy. It brings you to a place where you trust God's divine ability. You live, leaning not to your own understanding, but in all your ways, acknowledging Him.

The second observation is: Abraham and his men had to travel for three days to get where God wanted them to be, which suggests that some faith developments are attached to time. Upon their arrival at the set place, Abraham says to the accompanying companions, "stay here." Please, take note of this! Everyone can't go to where you are being called.

The next thing that Abraham tells the other men with him is, "The boy and I will return." The command that God gave was to offer Isaac as a Burnt offering. Remember, this requires that the entire sacrifice be destroyed. How, then, was Abraham able to say to their companions, "we will return?" Unless, Abraham was convinced that if God took Isaac's life, then God would give life back to Isaac. What a mighty God we serve! There is meaning, not just in what Abraham says (although it was profound), but also where he says it. They are headed up Mt. Moriah. Moriah means 'the place where the Lord will provide,' or 'the place where the Lord appears.'

When you are in over your head, get to a place where God can provide, a place where you give God the chance to become your Jehovah Jireh. In Genesis 22:14 of the Message Bible translation, the name of this place is translated as, *"God sees to it."* Faith requires that we see it to the end, so that God can see to it. The Lord is my light and my salvation. God's going to see to it! Stop worrying, stop fretting, and stop fussing. Just get to a place where God will see to it. Abraham prepares Isaac as a sacrifice, and was prepared to go all the way. You, too, must be prepared to go all the way with God. Knife in hand, Abraham was fully prepared to carry out the command of God. Something that I have come to know about God is that He has another hand. When you have exhausted all of your efforts, but your faith remains strong, have confidence that God will intervene. The Bible says, *"Having done all to stand, Stand!"* (Ephesians 6:13). When you have exhausted everything in your hand, trust in the Hand of God.

Bid Whist is a popular card game. The game requires partners to not only have knowledge of the game, but also complete confidence in one another.

So much so, that, without uttering a word, one partner can trust what's in the other partner's hand and have confidence in the outcome of the game. Abraham must have had the same kind of confidence in the hand of God, for, when he lifted his hand, the voice of God commanded, "stay your hand, Isaac's life is in my hands. I have prepared a ram in the bush."

Abraham's faith allowed him to reply to Isaac when the child asked, "Where is the sacrifice?" "The Lord God, before whom I have walked, will send His angel with you and me, and He will prosper my way," is essentially what Abraham told his son. The NIV translation says that God will "make your journey a success." Faith and obedience will cause you to believe that He, who has begun a good work in you, is able to bring it to its full fruition. Faith and obedience will cause you to experience the miraculous ability of God. You will live through the extraordinary provisions of God, matched only by His incredible timing. God will bring you out exactly when you need to come out, and exactly how you need to come out. We have numerous Bible stories that depict God's precise timing. The Hebrew boys in the fiery furnace, Daniel in the lion's den, and Jonah in the belly of the fish, all give credence to God's extraordinary ability to deliver us out of extraordinary circumstances. The steps of good persons are, indeed, ordered by God, especially when the outcome is designed to deepen your faith, or simply when you are over your head. There is a tendency to end the story here, but a deeper observation into verse fifteen brings us to the final observation.

This third and final observation is: The Lord said to Abraham, "by myself, I swear (I bring myself under complete obligation), blessing, I will bless thee (you), multiplying, I will multiply thee (you)." In other words, "Oh, how I will bless you! Oh, how I will bless you! Oh, how I will bless you!" The Lord's promises of blessings to Abraham are generational. Even today, believers who walk in faith are known as the seed of Abraham. There is yet a deeper meaning to the Abraham/Isaac story.

Abraham gives us a view, in the Old Testament, of what God will complete in the New Testament. Abraham was willing to sacrifice his son, by the command of God. The New Testament is a fulfillment of the Old Testament. The Burnt offering sacrifice merely shadows the living sacrifice of Jesus, the Son of God, who was the perfect sacrifice. How the hymns do so very well put into the song, the cries of our hearts:

> *"At the cross, at the cross, where I first saw the light and the burdens of my heart rolled away. It was there, by faith, I received my sight, and now I am happy all the day..."*

> *"There is a fountain filled with blood, drawn from Emmanuel's veins, and sinners plunge beneath the flow, lose all their guilty stains..."*

"Living, He loved me, dying, He saved me. Buried, He carried my sins away. Rising, He justified, freed me forever. One day, He's coming back, Glorious Day!"

It was the death of God's son that gave life to us. Abraham didn't have to do to Isaac what God had to do His son. *"For God so loved the world, that he gave his only begotten son, that whosoever believeth in Him will not perish but they shall have everlasting life"* (John 3:16). So know, that when you are in over your head and your ways still please God, the Lord will make a way somehow.

"No Limit"

A Sermon by VANETTA R. RATHER

Mark 7:31-35 *(Mixed versions used: NIV, NLT, AMP)*

*T*hen Jesus left the vicinity of Tyre and went through Sidon, down to the Sea of Galilee and into the region of the Decapolis. There some people brought to him a man who was deaf and mute and they begged him to place his hand on the man to heal him. Jesus led him to a private place away from the crowd. He put his fingers into the man's ears. Then, spitting onto his own fingers, he touched the man's tongue with the spittle. Jesus looked up to heaven and with a deep sigh said to him "Ephphatha" which means BE OPENED. And his ears were opened, his tongue was loosed and he began to speak distinctly and as he should.

At the end of every year I embrace a theme for the next year to help me grow a little more in faith. This year I embraced the theme "No Limit". "No Limit" seemed like just the theme I needed to keep me focused on getting to the next level. It was very fitting because I had reached a point in my life where I wanted to stretch my capacity to see God more like who God really is and less like what my limited, finite understanding made God out to be.

The more I embraced this theme of "No Limit", the more it spoke to me beyond my personal desires for growth. "No Limit" was becoming a message that was not just speaking to me, it was speaking to all of us... and I began to love what it was saying.

"No Limit" speaks to us about the supremacy of our God. It speaks of the boundless range, reach, and scope of God's dominion. This theme says to us that limitations and boundaries are foreign concepts to our God. It let's us know that there are no set perimeters to which God is confined. There are no restricted areas from which God is constrained. And there are no borders or territories that can operate outside or function independent of God's ruler-ship.

I love this theme "NO LIMIT" because it says to us that our God is the sole, autonomous ruler over everything there is. This theme eliminates any restrictions we would place on our God and reminds us that God is the Sovereign King of the entire universe! He has the power to do what he wants, when he wants and exactly how he wants. No one can deny him, no one can refuse him, and there is certainly no formidable opposition that can contest his authority. I'm talking about an all powerful God, unrestricted, unbound and unmatched... God is a "No Limit" God! And this is why I embrace this theme. I want to experience God in a No Limit kind of way.

I realize that I am probably not the only one who wants to have such an encounter with God. There must be others, like me, who don't want human limitations to block them from fully experiencing a God who holds and yields ALL POWER! So, God gave me a Word that will help us see Him beyond our *limited* ability, and begin to understand that we serve a God with *limitless* possibilities!

I love preaching about the limitless power of our God. I love that, in this topic, there are much deeper implications. You see, it's not just that we serve an all-powerful, limitless God. We serve an all-powerful, limitless God who desires to manifest his limitless power through the lives of his people. This, my brothers and my sisters, is our benefit. God is looking for some faithful people *through* whom he can display his wondrous works, show forth his sovereign strength, and demonstrate his awe-inspiring power. God is looking to do through us the greater works Jesus said we could do. This theme, "No Limit," hints not only to the endless possibilities of our God, but it hints to the endless possibilities of the people of God.

I believe God wants to do, in this earth, things that have yet to be seen. God is ready to show us the extent of his power. God is ready to act in ways that will blow our minds. God is ready to do the unthinkable, the unimaginable, and the unexpected. What we need to understand is this: our experiencing the "NO LIMIT" Power of God is not contingent on whether *God* is ready. It is contingent on whether *we* are ready. Are we ready to come out of the box, unchain ourselves from traditions, and flow with a God who has been rightly labeled "the God who acts in mysterious ways?"

I know our off the cuff answer to this question is "yes!" We love to sing that song, *"I'll say yes Lord. Yes to your will and to your way. I'll say yes, Lord. Yes, I will trust you and obey. When your Spirit speaks to me, with my whole heart, I'll agree, and my answer will be yes, Lord, yes."* But are we really open to the unpredictable, and often times peculiar ways of our God? This is a question we must ask ourselves, because our God is unique and He often goes against the grain of human reasoning and understanding. The only way we can experience the "No Limit" Power of God in our lives is to be opened to a God who operates, at times, within reason, but who also likes to shake it up a bit and do the strange and unheard of.

One thing I've come to realize is that being open is not the easiest thing for most people. Being open is difficult because it requires us to be vulnerable and exposed. It means we have to let our defenses down. We have to take chances and risk stepping into the unfamiliar and the unknown. This is very uncomfortable for most people. Most people prefer to play it safe. But it is impossible to play it safe and walk by faith at the same time. Living by faith is risky business. It requires a trust in God, even during the times when it makes no logical sense... ESPECIALLY during the times when it appears to be extremely illogical. If we want to experience the "No Limit" power of our God, we must be people who are opened to God, both when He makes complete common since and when he is doing the strange and unusual. Teachings in the gospel of Mark help free us to do this.

The gospel of Mark is a very appropriate gospel to help us see, firsthand, how Jesus works in unconventional and unexpected ways. This gospel notes early on that Jesus is constantly in conflict with the set expectations of the religious leaders of his day. In the early chapters of this gospel, Jesus is chastised by religious leaders for going against the established order by doing things like eating with tax collectors, healing someone on the Sabbath, and not demanding his disciples participate in a ritualistic fast. Because Jesus did not fall in line with the religious leaders, they took issue with him. They had a problem with the new stuff Jesus was doing.

The religious leaders believed that they had God all figured out. They were convinced that they knew everything about God, to the point that anything outside their realm of understanding was unacceptable. It's a very dangerous thing when the people of God think they have God locked, stocked, and barreled. It's a dangerous thing for us to think we are absolutely sure of God's next move. It is wise to remember that our ways are far from God's ways, and our thoughts are far from God's thoughts. When we think we know it all and attempt to pigeon-hole God to our limited understanding, we are only denying ourselves the opportunity to experience the fullness of what an all-powerful God can do. We have to constantly make sure we are open. The people of God have a tendency to get stuck in the usual, and

God wants to sometimes flex His muscle and do the unusual. Our God is not predictable! Often, we look for God to come through the front door, but here comes God through the window. We see this in the Word.

In the seventh chapter of Mark, verse 32 talks about some people bringing a man who needed to be healed to Jesus. The text doesn't say who the people were, but they must have been people of faith for they believed Jesus had the power to heal. But what stood out to me was that these people told Jesus exactly how to heal the man. They asked Jesus to "lay his hands on the man" so that he can be healed. They had their own idea about how Jesus should do what they needed Him to do. They assumed because they had witnessed Jesus' healing this way in the past. They were stuck on the methods Jesus used previously. I believe this is how we sometimes get stuck. God isn't looking to do that same ole' stale stuff over and over, God is looking to do a new thing. God gave <u>fresh</u> manna from heaven daily because he didn't want his people eating stale, left over manna. I believe God still desires to give fresh manna. But when we allow what God did in the past to dictate our future, we hinder the new and radical things God wants to do today.

Now, after the people brought this man to Jesus and told him how to heal him, Jesus just ignored them. I don't know about you, but when I come up with my own high and lofty plans for life, I'm so glad that Jesus just ignores me. Then, Jesus took the man away from the crowd that had their own set expectations. If we are going to experience this "No

Limit" power in our lives, we have to let Jesus take us away from those who want things their way and could care less about God's way.

Jesus took the man away in private. In private, Jesus doesn't have to compete for our attention. In private, Jesus can deal with us one on one. In private, Jesus speaks to us about destiny and purpose. Jesus longs to meet us in private. But when we meet Jesus in private, this is where we really need to be open. We have to be open when we get alone with Jesus, because it is often in our alone time with Him where Jesus unveils His strange plans.

Noah was alone when God told him to build a huge boat. Sarah was alone when she overheard she could bare children at 90. Moses was alone when God told him he would defeat Pharaoh. Zachariah was alone when God told him he would have a son in his old age. And the Virgin Mary was alone when God told her she would give birth to God. These were all strange plans. God still wants to do some strange and unusual things! If we want to experience these things, we've got to be like the man in the text who received healing. This man allowed Jesus to take him away from the crowd.

This man didn't box Jesus in and dictate to Him how to do what needed to be done. This man was just willing to be a recipient of the "No Limit" power of Jesus. He didn't care how Jesus healed him. He just wanted to be healed. This ought to be our testimony. We should not care how Jesus does whatever he does in our lives—we just need to be open to whatever he's doing. Contrary to how the people in the text expected Jesus to heal the man, Jesus did something strange and unusual. Jesus throughst his fingers into the man's ears and took some spit out of his mouth and put in on the man's tongue.

What I believe God is asking is "are you open enough to be able to handle the strange, unusual, and uncomfortable things God wants to do with you?" I wonder, if we were in this man's position, how many of us would remain silent over Jesus putting spit on our tongue? How many of us are choosing to remain where we are over the challenge of embracing the unfamiliar and unconventional ways of our God? How many of us forfeit the blessings and new levels in God, because we feel more safe doing the familiar than we do walking by faith. Faith is about trusting a God who acts outside our realm of reasoning. If you don't like taking risks, then you've hooked up with the wrong God! You may need to go and worship a passive god who doesn't care what you do, because the True and Living God expects you to take some risks!

After Jesus put his fingers in the man's ears and put spit on his tongue, he looked up to heaven and took a deep sigh and said "BE OPENED!" Now, we need to really pay attention to what Jesus said. I believe Jesus is intentional and selective about the Words he uses. He has to be, because words are meant to perform. Jesus' Words come to life. It was by His Words that the world was created. There is power in his Words.

I noticed that Jesus didn't just say "open," like this was to be a one time thing. Jesus said "be opened." The word "be" is significant. "Be" is a helping verb, or a state of being verb, and it is used here in the present tense. The word "be" helps out the verb "open" by telling us the state in which we ought to live. This makes it clear to us that "opened" is to be a continuous state of existing for the people of God. It's not that we are to be open when it's comfortable and convenient, but God wants us to continually be opened. Isn't if funny how the stranger a thing is, or the more ridiculous a thing sounds, or the more something stretches us out of our comfort zones, the more likely it is to be God.

But know that it pays to be in this position. Verse 35 says "instantly" the man could hear perfectly and his tongue was freed so he could speak plainly. This is what being opened to God will do for us. Being opened ensures that we hear perfectly *from* God so we can speak freely *for* God. God needs for his people to be able to clearly hear his still, small, unique voice. A voice that is different, peculiar and unconventional. A voice that defies logic and reason. A voice that sometimes gives unrealistic and unbelievable instructions. God needs for us to hear him perfectly so we can speak freely and proclaim boldly, to a dying world, that there is a God who has limitless power. The power to change any situation. The power to heal AIDS and HIV, the power to end homelessness, the power to even end the senseless wars. If God's people would be opened to hear from God and speak for God, we would see a real manifestation of God's limitless power in this earth.

Jesus said we would do greater works than the works that he did. Just what kind of works did Jesus do? Jesus was in the liberation business! Jesus' work centered around bringing abundant living, justice, freedom, and salvation to a world that was set to self-destruct. There is a dying world that needs for the people who claim to love Jesus to continue to do the work of Jesus. Jesus wants this work to continue, but this can only happen when God's people embrace and are opened to change. I know change is a hard word for us to embrace, but we stand to lose so much when we are unable to go with God's flow.

When God's people are open to coming out of the box, doing new things, and going into new territories, God will not only change and transform our individual lives, but because we are foolish enough to trust God, He'll use us in mighty ways to impact this world and advance His Kingdom. This is the *true* benefit of being hooked up with a "No Limit" God. We get blessed, and then we get the privilege of being able to turn around and blessing someone else. This will happen because when God's "No Limit" power touches our lives in a real way, it's contagious to the point that we can't help but pass the blessing on.

This is exactly what happened in the text with the people that tried to tell Jesus how to heal the man. After they witnessed the results of allowing Jesus to do something outside their expectations, not only were they changed but they began to spread the good news in hopes of changing the lives of others. Verse 36 says that Jesus even told them not to tell anyone, but they had a case of the "can't help its." Has God ever done anything for you and you couldn't help but tell it? Has God ever blessed you in an unusually strange way to the point that you just couldn't keep it to yourself? This crowd couldn't help but tell about the wonder working power of Jesus. They were first hand witnesses that being open to the strange workings of an all powerful God could do far more for them than they could ever think or imagine. They learned to trust God beyond their realm of reasoning.

This is what being opened is all about. It's about trusting Jesus in season and out of season. It's about trusting Jesus when we can't make heads or tails of our situation. It's about trusting Jesus when all hell breaks loose in our lives. Just why do we trust Jesus, even when he acts strange and unusual? I'm glad you asked. We trust Jesus simply because of what the crowd proclaimed in verse 37, *"everything he does is wonderful."*

We can trust Jesus and be open to whatever he wants to do, because everything he does is wonderful! He heals wonderfully, he delivers divinely, he orchestrates effectively, and he transforms triumphantly. Everything He does is wonderful! It may be strange at times, it may be unusual, but it is all together WONDERFUL! This is even proven with the cross. The Bible says the cross is foolishness to the world and God purposely used what was considered foolish to bring about redemption and salvation.

The cross was a shameful death, and some probably thought this had to be the worse salvation plan ever conceived. Just look at how crazy it sounds: the All-Powerful, Sovereign, Eternal God of the universe... dies. This sounds insane! This is crazy, absurd thinking! I can imagine the crowd, as they witnessed the crucifixion, shaking their heads as Jesus was being nailed to the cross as some murmured "this was a dumb plan." When the soldiers pierced him in the side and put a crown of thorns on his head, I can hear the half-stifled doubt in the crowd, "sure enough, the plan has failed!" Then, over the course of two days, while Jesus was divinely napping in an old borrowed tomb, I'm sure that many went looking for a plan B. But I'm so glad that our ways are far from His ways. I'm so glad God doesn't think and reason like we do. We have the testimony that although his salvation plan was a strange plan, although it was an unusual plan, it was a **successful** plan. On the third day, Jesus rose from the grave with POWER. Not just any kind of earthly power… NO LIMIT Power!

If we are opened to God, we get full access to that No Limit Power! If we can be opened to the unconventional salvation plan, then, surely, we can condition ourselves to be continuously opened to whatever our "No Limit" God wants to do through and in us. We can be opened because we now know, and are certainly convinced, like the crowd in the text, that *Everything He Does is Wonderful!*

"I'm Tired of Being Sick & Tired"

A Sermon by TRENACE N. RICHARDSON

Nehemiah 1:1-11 (New Living Translation)

"These are the memoirs of Nehemiah son of Hacaliah. In late autumn, in the month of Kislev, in the twentieth year of King Artaxerxes' reign, I was at the fortress of Susa. Hanani, one of my brothers, came to visit me with some other men who had just arrived from Judah. I asked them about the Jews who had returned there from captivity and about how things were going in Jerusalem. They said to me, "Things are not going well for those who returned to the province of Judah. They are in great trouble and disgrace. The wall of Jerusalem has been torn down, and the gates have been destroyed by fire." When I heard this, I sat down and wept. In fact, for days I mourned, fasted, and prayed to the God of heaven. Then I said, "O LORD, God of heaven, the great and awesome God who keeps his covenant *of unfailing love with those who love him and obey his commands, listen to my prayer! Look down and see me praying night and day for your people Israel. I confess that we have sinned against you. Yes, even my own family and I have sinned! We have sinned terribly by not obeying the commands, decrees, and regulations that you gave us through your servant Moses. "Please remember what you told your servant Moses: 'If you are unfaithful to me, I will scatter you among the nations. But if you return to me and obey my commands and live by them, then even if you are exiled to the ends of the earth, I will bring you back to the place I have chosen for my name to be honored.' "The people you rescued by your great power and strong hand are your servants. O Lord, please hear my prayer! Listen to the prayers of those of us who delight in honoring you. Please grant me success today by making the king favorable to me. Put it into his heart to be kind to me." In those days I was the king's cup-bearer. O Lord, please hear my prayer! Listen to the prayers of those of us who delight in honoring you. Please grant me success today by making the king favorable to me. Put it into his heart to be kind to me." In those days I was the king's cup-bearer."*

I am one of those women who grew up in church. My mother insisted that we attend church every week, and I came to love and appreciate my Pentecostal COGIC (Church of God In Christ) church experience. I was accustomed to, and accepting of, the long worship services, the long prayer lines, the second or third offerings, and the seventy minute sermon. I adhered to the "Sunday's best" dress code, complete with stockings, slip, church hat, lap cloth, and matching patent-leather shoes and bag.

It was when I went off to college that I realized, my specific church history, with all its pomp and circumstance, did not prevent me from becoming the fast freshman who lost my virginity to the first super-senior who was able to convince me that I was his one and only… when, in reality, I was his one of several. I can't speak for anyone else, but my history of being in church all week, every week, did not keep me from falling for, and giving myself to, the same type of guy, one right after the other, even after I started serving in a ministry.

I tried to compensate for my weakness in relationships by becoming an overachiever in every other area of my life – education, work, pageants, and ministry. I realized the truth: attending a holiness church did not make me holy, standing in long prayer lines did not cause me to stand up for myself when it came to having sex, and wearing my Sunday best did not cause me to give God my best. So, once I got out of college, I started looking for a church that would teach me not only how to dance, shout, and speak in tongues inside the church building, but how to live a godly life outside it as well.

On my quest to find a church home, I visited many churches, and found myself growing tired of the same old, same old. Everything I encountered was so predictable and nothing resembled the powerful, life-changing experience I longed for. I grew tired of people hugging me and smiling one minute, then turning around and talking about me in the next. I grew tired of the choir refusing to stop singing. I grew tired of preachers holding me hostage until they finally got the entire congregation on their feet, dancing and shouting: just to make themselves feel like they accomplished something awesome in the service. I grew tired of worship leaders making me feel guilty if I didn't do everything they directed me to do. I grew tired of prayer lines that promised a right now blessing if I brought $20 up with me. I grew tired of the fashion-show-like competition, which fueled the vain process of deciding what to wear to church every week. I grew sick and tired of putting on the required "church face" so everyone would think that I was "blessed and highly favored," "too blessed to be stressed," and "glad to be in the land of the living," when, inside, I really felt broken, hopeless, fearful, and lonely.

I wondered why the church, which was supposed to be my saving grace, was the place that left me feeling the most drained, overworked, underpaid, unimpressed, and uninspired. I was sick and tired of church as usual! So, I kept up my search for the kind of church I knew I needed, and, in the meantime, I started talking to a few close girlfriends about my frustrations. I came to realize that they, too, were feeling the same way about churches they had come across. They, too, were feeling uninspired and unimpressed by church and church folk. Most of all, we were all looking for something more, something deeper, and something meaningful. We didn't plan to abandon church altogether. We just wanted a safe place to express ourselves. We needed to figure out how we could help the church become the true 'safe haven' it is supposed to be.

So, I decided to pull all of my girlfriends together for a meeting, on a monthly basis. We started meeting at my house, and we would talk for hours about ourselves, our church, and our ministry experiences. We discussed how we were balancing church and family, and what God was revealing to us about our lives and our relationships. We did it faithfully for a long while, and enjoyed ourselves so much, until we decided we were being selfish keeping this type of fellowship to ourselves. My girlfriends and I decided to hold an annual summit (officially named, the Women in Ministry Summit) for other women who serve in ministry, and who may also have needed opportunities to be encouraged, equipped, and empowered to keep giving, despite their frustrations.

The Summit needed to be an authentic, transparent place where women could talk about anything and not be judged or condemned for it. So, we decided to invite some seasoned, down-to-earth women in ministry to come, listen to us, and answer some of our questions. It has been four years running now, and it is an awesome success.

My reason for sharing that is, for me, Young Women in Ministry, Inc. and the Women in Ministry Summit were birthed out of my pain and the pain of others who were sick and tired of the way we saw things done around us. During the process of growing with these women, I even found a church that met all of my needs, in the area of spiritual growth and transformation, in a real, authentic, and inspiring environment. My church may not be perfect, but I am convinced that I can grow there.

Since starting a ministry to address some of the issues that other women in my position may face, it has become evident that there are still so many frustrated people out there. People are sick and tired of the church being more a part of the problem than the solution. This is why it's still my burning desire to share Christ with as many people as I can, in a transparent, creative, authentic, honest, and powerful ways, to help balance out all of the other stuff we experience in ministry.

Bill Hybels (2007) calls the frustration I just described, a "holy discontent." A holy discontent is the frustration one feels that leads them to the very thing for which God wants to use them. I'm willing to bet that I am not the only one who has experienced a holy discontent. Maybe you have experienced it in the areas that I just described, and maybe it's because of church and church folk that you want to pull your hair out. Maybe you are an educator, or a parent, sick and tired of failing schools, and you know there has to be a more effective way of reaching our children. Maybe you are sick of tired of seeing the way the poor and homeless are treated. Maybe you are tired of watching young girls grow up too fast, giving their goodies away before they're old enough to responsibly open up their candy store. Maybe you are sick and tired of seeing marriages crumble around you, or seeing singles living lonely, and defeated lives.

I need you to consider what it is that has made you, or is continually making you, sick and tired, because I want you to know that whatever that thing is, it's probably your holy discontent. That is the area where God wants to see you work to positively impact this world for Him. Think about it. What is the thing that gets your blood boiling? Who does it affect? What frustrates you about it? I need you to take some time to truly think about it. Do not simply get sick and tired of it, I need you to get tired of BEING sick and tired. I need you to get so tired of seeing what frustrates you, that you decide to do something about it.

As church women, we are used to encouragement and motivation coming to us, letting us know it's going to be alright, what God has for us is for us, and that our house, our car, and our blessing are all on the way. While all of that is true, there is another level of spiritual maturity where God would like to take us. This level is where we are encouraged simply by walking in our divine purpose. This level is where we are encouraged by seeing others being blessed by the gifts that God has given to us. This is the level where we have the opportunity to make some real, positive changes to advance the Kingdom of God.

See, it's the "little girl" kind of faith that allows you to trust God only when everything is going your way. I'm looking for the full-grown women, who, even when going through hard times, are still willing to figure out how God wants to use them to advance His will and His work here on earth. It's the little girl who only wants to do what is comfortable and easy and familiar. It's the full-grown woman who says, "I will step out of my comfort zone to do what God is calling me to do, because I recognize that if I don't, I won't be able to rest and find peace. If I don't, my holy discontent will keep me frustrated, until I get tired of being sick and tired of what I see!"

The question now is, once you decide that you are fed up and you want to satisfy your holy discontent, what do you do? Once you get tired of being sick and tired, how do you do something about it? Well, my best "how to" models come from the Word of God, so let me use a biblical example to paint this picture clearly.

There is a man in the Bible named Nehemiah, who wrote about his life. He writes that he was a cupbearer to the king—meaning, he lived in the palace, and tested the king's drinks to make sure they were not poisonous. Now this may sound like a dangerous, cruddy job, but the truth is, there was a definite level of prestige that came with working directly for the government. There were some automatic benefits to it. Especially since most of his people were jobless, homeless, and in great distress. Working for the king as the cupbearer was better than what most had during his day. I liken it today, with having a good government job, or being a computer technician, or working as an administrative assistant. While these jobs may not be the most ideal, maybe because of pay or long hours or the people you work with, but in hard economic times, when so many are jobless and losing homes, the job you have will do just fine for now.

The problem with that mentality, for us and for Nehemiah, is that 'cupbearer' is not what he was created to do. Don't get me wrong, it was in God's plan for him to be the cupbearer, because if he had not been the cupbearer, he would not have been in a position to help his people. So, yes, there was purpose and reason behind him taking that job when he did, but, evidently, cupbearing did not address his holy discontent (the frustration one feels that leads them to the very thing God wants to use them to do).

I know this, because in Nehemiah 1:1-4, when he ran into his brother and asked how things were going in Jerusalem for his people, who had survived the exile, he broke down and cried upon hearing the news. His brother told him that those in exile were in great trouble and distress, and the gates of Jerusalem had been broken down and burned with fire. When Nehemiah heard that his home was in ruins, he wept. The reason for his tears, I believe, is evident in his prayer. Not only was he upset about how his people were being treated, but he also knew that his people, the Jews, proclaimed to serve the one true God, were now living in ruins. Now, it must have appeared, to all of the ungodly nations, that his God was powerless and incapable of delivering them. This made him weep. Nehemiah, like many of us desired to make a change and take a stance for things that he knew in his heart was the right thing(s) to do for the people and on behalf of God. Nehemiah shows us three things that we must do, if we truly desire to serve the people and follow the urging of our Lord.

1. <u>FIND YOUR HOLY DISCONTENT!</u> Nehemiah shows us that no matter where we are in life, no matter what we are doing, or what kind of job we have, we have to be open and ready to discover our holy discontent. Amid the hustle and bustle of what you do everyday - work, school, children, church, clubs, meetings, and relationships - do you know what causes you to weep? What breaks your heart when you see it? If you don't know, be

prayerful about God revealing it to you. Then, be
open to finding it, because God will show it to you.
Even though that job you are working pays the bills,
if it does not address your holy discontent, there is
something else, or something more, you are supposed
to be doing with your life.

I am not advocating quitting your job and
becoming irresponsible. In fact, Nehemiah did not
quit his job! He simply asked the king if he could use
some of his leave. We find time for what we make
time for, and I am challenging us to make sure that
before we leave this earth we have made time to do
the things God has designed and fueled us to do.
What good is it to retire from a great government job,
or a good company position after years of service,
if we never found time to discover what is was that
God wanted us to accomplish while we were on this
earth?

2. <u>PRAY AND ASK GOD FOR FAVOR!</u> Not
only did the bad news make Nehemiah cry, but it
also caused him to pray and ask God for favor, as
he made the decision to act on Jerusalem's behalf
by speaking to the king. Once you find your holy
discontent, pray and ask God for favor as you move
toward acting on it. In order for Nehemiah to go and
help those in Jerusalem, he knew he would need the
king's blessing and help.

Asking God for favor is one of the wisest things
you can do, before you venture out to act on your holy
discontent. God's favor will take you farther than you
could ever go by yourself. His favor will speak on
your behalf when you don't know what to say. His
favor will move obstacles out of your way that you

would never be able to move on your own. God's favor is more precious than the money you get paid or the high-titled position you strive to attain. Have you ever experienced the favor of God wherein He put you in places, gave you things, and afforded you opportunities that had nothing to do with your skill set, your expertise, your credentials, or your resume? It came directly from the hand of God.

Please, don't let others make you feel bad about the favor of God. As many have said before me, "favor ain't fair!" This is not about everyone of us getting the same exact thing, this is about each of us getting a *tailor made* blessing from God, so we can do whatever it is He has called us to do, individually. First, you have to find your holy discontent. Then, you have to ask God for favor to bless you in your pursuit to address your holy discontent.

I don't have the space and time to really detail all of the ways God favored Nehemiah with the king, so, please, go there, and study it in your personal time. Just know that, because of Nehemiah's position as cupbearer, God placed it on the king's heart to grant him provision and protection while he went to see about Jerusalem. The king gave Nehemiah men and supplies to take with him, to help provide what he would need on his journey. The favor didn't stop there. The king also gave Nehemiah Royal Decrees that he could show to anyone along the way who might be hostile towards him for coming through their land. Because Nehemiah endured being the king's cupbearer, the king's favor promised provision and protection, as Nehemiah moved into what God was calling him to do.

I want you to know that there is a reason why you have been where you are for so long. There is a reason why you have been led to be as faithful and dedicated as you have been. That reason is, when you do venture out and begin to act on what God is calling you to do, you should be able to go back to the people you built relationships with, and networked with, and find provision and protection, because God's favor is on your life. Favor ain't fair, but favor is fun, if you work it right and are willing to fight to keep it!

3. <u>FIGHT FOR YOUR HOLY DISCONTENT!</u> The last part of Nehemiah's story that I will share with you is that he had to fight for his holy discontent. What you find in the next several chapters is that Nehemiah had to rally his people to help him build the wall, which wasn't easy. He faced opposition from the enemies of the Jews, who wanted to keep the Jews oppressed and in ruins. Then, when they finally got the wall up, they had to deal with their enemies to keep it protected. This goes to show that once you discover your holy discontent and you ask God for favor to address it, there is still much work that needs to be done to make it happen and keep it going. You have to be willing to make time for, plan for, invest in, and fight for what you know God is calling you to do.

Don't give up on it when times are hard and they require you to keep your 9 to 5. Work on it after hours, during your lunch breaks, and on the weekends. Don't give it up just because you see someone else doing something similar. God gave it to you, so do it the way He gave it to YOU! Don't stop working on it because you don't have any extra income right now (extra is relative). Sacrifice for it, save that Starbucks money or that movie money or that manicure/pedicure money for several months to get the equipment or the license or the website that you need to get started. Don't give up on your God-given dream! Fight for it! Get a warrior's attitude about it. Decide that you can't die with this dream in your heart; you've got to see it realized. You won't die wishing you had done it; you are going to do it! You have to decide that you are so sick and tired of seeing this thing in your head, you won't rest until you see it manifested in the natural. You have to get "tired" of being sick and tired. That's when you are ready to fight for it.

I would like to encourage you by telling you a story about how mother turtles bury their eggs way up shore, knowing that when the eggs hatch, they won't be there to help the baby turtles make it to the water. Once they hatch, the babies have to struggle by themselves to make it to their destination. It's on that hard, tedious journey that they build up strength in their legs and strengthen their lungs, so that by the time they make it to the water, they are strong enough to swim successfully. If the mother turtle had simply laid her eggs right by the water, they would not have developed the adequate strength in the struggle and would have drowned when they hit the water. There is success in our struggles. May God not allow you to rest until you discover, pursue, and fulfill your holy discontent.

"Say It Until You See It"

A Sermon by SANDRA RILEY

Mark 10:46-52 (King James Version)

"**A**nd they came to Jericho: and as he went out of Jericho with his disciples and a great number of people, blind Bartimaeus, the son of Timaeus, sat by the highway side begging. And when he heard that it was Jesus of Nazareth, he began to cry out, and say, "Jesus, thou son of David, have mercy on me." And many charged him that he should hold his peace: but he cried the more a great deal, "Thou son of David, have mercy on me." And Jesus stood still, and commanded him to be called. And they call the blind man, saying unto him, "Be of good comfort, rise; he calleth thee." And he, casting away his garment, rose, and came to Jesus. And Jesus answered and said unto him, "What wilt thou that I should do unto thee?" The blind man said unto him, "Lord, that I might receive my sight." And Jesus said unto him," Go thy way; thy faith hath made thee whole." And *immediately he received his sight, and followed Jesus in the way".*

Mark 11:23 (King James Version)

"For verily I say unto you, That whosoever shall say unto this mountain, Be thou removed, and be thou cast into the sea; and shall not doubt in his heart, but shall believe that those things which he saith shall come to pass; he shall have whatsoever he saith."

Blind Bartimaeus, the son of Timaeus, was doing what he was accustomed to doing: sitting by the roadside begging, asking alms of all who passed by. The Bible says that when he heard it was Jesus of Nazareth passing by, he began to cry out more, a great deal more. He began to open up his mouth and shout out, "Jesus, son of David, have mercy on me." The text leads us to believe, he must have heard something about what Jesus was able to do. Perhaps Word of Jesus' healing power had reached him. Surely, Bartimaeus had heard something about Jesus' delivering power. He must have also heard that it wouldn't cost him anything to be delivered and healed by the man they call Jesus. He trusted that if he just believed Jesus was able, then Jesus could and would meet all of his needs.

As Bartimaeus was sitting there, and heard Jesus passing by, it's as if he realized that this was his chance to be healed by the Master Healer. I can hear him saying to himself, "I'm not comfortable with the state that I'm in anymore. I don't want to beg for money all of my life. If Jesus, the one who can heal me, is here, I can get my needs met today."

That day, on the side of the road, Bartimaeus made a decision to stop looking to people to be the source of what he needed to survive. That day, he decided to no longer be comfortable sitting down, begging to survive. Bartimaeus switched sources as he cried out to Jesus for a miracle.

Romans 10:17 lets us know that *"faith cometh by hearing, and hearing by the Word of God."* You've got to hear, and continuously hear, God's Word, for your faith to yield divine results. If you have not heard what the Lord has said concerning your situation, you have not heard the last of the matter. You can't depend on what friends are saying; you have to get a Word from the Lord. If you're facing a time where bad news seems to be coming at you from everywhere you turn, so much so that it's beginning to dictate the choices you make, this is your message. It's time to make up your mind that, in spite of the bad news you're hearing, you're going to keep moving, and keep believing that God is going to help you. Even though you may have heard many bad reports, many negative words, God wants you to know that until you hear what he has to say, you haven't heard the last word about the situation. So, open up your ears and listen to what the Father is saying to you and your situation.

The Word of the Lord says that once Bartimaeus heard, his faith was activated. His faith in Jesus as his way-maker, his deliverer, his prayer answerer, was activated. Bartimeaus' faith in the power of the Lord is what made it possible for him to receive the power of Jesus that sets the captives free. That same power is what is ready to snatch you back when you feel like you're on the verge of losing your mind. Notice that, once Bartimeaus heard and believed, he opened his mouth and began to speak for his heart's desire. Hebrews 11:3 lets us know that there is creative power in the Word of God. The Bible says that *"through faith we understand that the worlds were framed by the Word of God, so that things which are seen were not made of things which do appear."* The world looked invisible, but the Word that was *spoken* changed what was seen. In Genesis, God says, *"Let there be..."* and then there is. He didn't look at darkness and say, "Ooh, it's dark out here." He didn't tell the situation what it was, He spoke to the situation from what He wanted it to be. He looked at the darkness and said, "Let there be light." That same power is what He has put inside of us, via His Word.

Someone needs to take hold of the creative power of words, and when you walk into that house of chaos, turmoil and confusion, don't get involved in what you see. Speak into the situation and call it what you desire for it to be. You must be bold and decree to your chaos, "let there be peace, in the name of Jesus." The world was brought forth, brought into existence, by the spoken Word of God. Knowing the creative power in your words, don't expect the enemy to just sit back and let you go to work creating order and peace in your life. As Bartimaeus began to speak, many charged him that he should hold his peace. That's really just a nice way of saying, "they told him to shut up." The crowd was trying to discourage Bartimaeus from seeking the Lord for his healing.

You have to understand that when you make up in your mind to use the Word of God to reframe your world, the enemy is going to step in and try to make you shut up. Understand that, regardless of what the devil says, you must be motivated enough to open your mouth and say what God says. The devil knows that if he can get you to shut up, you will remain in the same defeated state. I want to challenge you to break the cycle of defeat. Quit sitting there in silence, allowing the devil to wreak havoc in your life. Quit sitting back, looking like you've been sucking on lemons. Come out of your depressed, oppressed, and obsessive state of defeat to open up your mouth and decree what God has spoken over your life.

If you can just open up your mouth and say what God says, you can change some things. That is why, when trouble comes, the first thing the devil wants you to do is be quiet. He knows that you shape your destiny by the words of your confession.

Let's examine some of what the Word tells us. Psalm 107:20 says, *"He sent his word and healed them and delivered them from their destruction."* Psalm 81:10 says, *"I am the Lord your God, who brought you out of the Land of Egypt, open your mouth wide and I will fill it."* This is the day for you to decree a good thing for yourself, in the name of Jesus. My beloved, you need to open your mouth, and decree your future. Speak forth what you are expecting God to do for you, in and through you. You must be willing to decree that you are going to see even greater glory, and that your ending will be better than your beginning. You must open your mouth and decree what God has spoken over you.

God expects you to open up your mouth and shift what's going on in your life. If you have the faith-God has the power!

Do you see that no matter what the people in the crowd said to Bartimaeus, he did not stop pursuing Jesus. He realized that the ones who were trying to shut him up weren't the ones who needed to be set free from blindness. They had no say in his healing, and Bartimaeus had enough revealed knowledge to know that he had to push past those who were trying to stop him from getting to his healer. You must open your mouth and speak what God says. Job 22:28 says, *"Thou shall also decree a thing."* You can open your mouth and speak it, and "it shall be established." When declarations of the Word are proclaimed over you, over your situation, over your family, your finances, and your health, the Word is then activated to strengthen your spirit.

The Lord says through Isaiah in chapter 55 and verse 11, *"So shall my word be that goes forth out of my mouth, it shall not return unto me void, but it shall accomplish that which I please, and it shall prosper in the thing whereto I sent it."* The Word is going to accomplish exactly what it is sent out to do. The devil knows that there is power in the Word of God and that is why he wants to keep you out of God's Word and he wants to keep God's Word out of you. You've been bound long enough; the challenge is for you to speak your way out of that bondage. You've been sick long enough; the challenge is for you to speak your way into healing. You've been broke, busted, and disgusted long enough; your challenge is to now open your mouth and speak your way into good stewardship and prosperity.

You've got say it until you see it. Just knowing what the Bible says isn't enough; you have to let it come out of your mouth. In James 3:3, the Bible explains to us how a bit in the mouth of a horse gives you the ability to control the whole body of the horse. As a young girl, I was able to witness this firsthand. In the summers, my family would go to the South to visit my grandmother and other relatives. I always liked having a chance to ride the horses. When learning how to ride, the first things I needed to know were how to make the horse go, stop, and turn. My family taught me that when you want a horse to turn in a certain direction, you must pull the reins in that direction. The reins are connected to the bit in the mouth of the horse. That bit puts an amount of pressure on the mouth of the horse that allows you to control the whole animal. Keep in mind, as you allow all kinds of destruction to leave your mouth, it is your mouth which has the power to pull the entire self in one direction or another.

You may even be in a situation where it looks like things will not, or can not, change. You have to say the change you desire to see, and keep saying it until you see it. You have to keep putting pressure on your tongue. Control your tongue, and see if your life starts moving in the direction that your words are leading it. Keep decreeing the Word of God until your situation turns. What you say will frame your world. Bartimaeus kept saying what he was seeking from God. Even after others tried to shut him up, he kept crying out to Jesus. Bartimaeus didn't want money; he wanted mercy to change his situation.

Are you ready for a change in your situation? Not just a shout, or a good feeling, but a change. Bartimaeus cried out until Jesus stopped walking, stood still, and commanded him to come. The Word of the Lord says that Bartimaeus wore an outer garment. This outer garment is what distinguished him as a blind person and gave him the right to beg for money. Notice that as soon as Jesus called for Bartimaeus, he cast away that outer garment FIRST, and THEN got up to go to Jesus. What a showcase of his faith. Bartimaeus knew, from the moment Jesus called him, that he was not going to be Blind Bartimaeus any longer!

I can imagine Bartimaeus being asked, "What are you doing man? You are throwing your coat down?" He recognized that it was not just any coat; it was a beggar's coat. However, Bartimaeus, on his way to stand before Jesus, had no more need for a beggar's coat. Can you hear his faith saying, "I'm about to be free from this bondage of begging, so I'm not going to wait until I enter into His presence to look like who I'm going to be, I can look like it right now."

Are you ready to look like you have the victory now? Are you ready to look like you are already healed? Are you ready to look like your way has already been made? When Bartimaeus stood in the presence of Jesus, Jesus asked him, "What would thou that I should do unto thee?" Jesus waited on him to open his mouth and say what his faith had the capacity to receive. When you open your mouth, you are releasing your faith into the atmosphere. Proverbs 18:21 says, *"Death and life are in the power of the tongue; and they that love it shall eat the fruit thereof."*

You are forming and creating your world with your words. That is why you must watch what you say. Start speaking life over your children, over your marriage, and over every dead situation that is in your life. Stop speaking death and negativity. Know what you want, and ask God for it! Bartimaeus received exactly what he had faith to receive. Place a demand on the power that God has made available to you. God is waiting on you to place a demand upon heaven. Ask Him to do something for you that no one else can do for you. Ask Him to repair something that only He can fix. Ask Him to make straight what no one else can unbend.

Once you've asked, even if you don't see it manifest right away, keep speaking it, because you know it's done. If your declaration is lining up with the Word and will of God, you will see results. In Jeremiah 1:12, God tells us that, *"I will hasten my word to perform it."* The word "hasten" in the text is also translated "watch over." God watches over His Word, to do what it says. This is a message for you who are ready for a change, and who are ready for a turnaround.

Have you been blinded by your trouble, blinded by your sickness, blinded by despair, blinded by discouragement, or blinded by the cares of the world? God is saying to you "just say it, until you see it turn around." Open your mouth, this is your day for a turnaround, this is the day for your life to be changed. Declare that this is your day for answers to be received. This is your day to tell the devil, "Back up, get out of my way, in the name of Jesus. I'm coming through...in the name of the Lord." Say It Until You See It!

"Change: A Necessity for Your Breakthrough"

A Sermon by ELIZABETH SAPP JONES

Genesis 38:27 (New International Version)

"*When the time came for her to give birth, there were twin boys in her womb.*"

On Tuesday, November 4th 2008, a historic moment was witnessed throughout the world, as a change manifested itself upon the political scene of this country. The election of Senator Barack Hussein Obama as the 44th President of the United States of America, becoming the country's first African-American man to hold that office, was proof that, "with God, nothing shall be impossible." As I watched the television, with tears flowing down my checks, I knew, with some certainty, that I was not alone as I attempted to digest the wave of emotions that engulfed me as this surreal and monumental event unfolded before my very eyes. I could not help but think of the history of my people, which included the middle passage and the unbridled brutality of 400 years of slavery that fostered rape, castration, and family annihilation. My mind churned as the memories of one period of dehumanizing experiences was followed by the memories of what was birthed from the lingering spirits of that prior period: Jim Crow, segregation, assassinations, lynchings, cross burnings, classism, red bordering, redistricting, and the ever present glass ceiling. It was such juxtaposition within my thoughts as I sat, paralyzed, watching on the screen before me. Unbeknownst to millions, the change that took place on that night began on a cold night some 21 months earlier.

On February 10, 2007, the junior senator from Illinois announced his candidacy for the highest office of the land. Many laughed, sneered, and thought that it was an exercise in futility. Yet, undaunted by his critics, Senator Obama ran his political campaign on the simple slogan, "Change, Yes We Can." And change, we did. Little by little, bit by bit, a momentum began to swell in this nation. The idea of a black man running for the highest office in the land, began to resonate with not just blacks, but whites, browns, reds and yellows as well. It is remarkable that, with everything that has taken place throughout the history of this country, and all of the pervasive, systemic, and institutional racism that continues to prevail today, a change has come. I declare unto you, however, that this kind of change can only be attributed to the work of the Holy Spirit.

The Holy Spirit, the magnanimous gift given to us by God on the Day of Pentecost, was offered to us, not so that we would stay the same or remain in the same old tired condition, but so that we could BREAKTHROUGH obstacles, BREAKUP traditions and BREAKOUT of mindsets that keep us bound and limited. God gave us the Holy Spirit so that, instead of dying in mediocrity, we would give birth to the innate POWER given to us by God, through the Holy Spirit, to change, not just ourselves, but the world around us.

While it is true that an African-American man was elected to the office of the President, it is also true that real change does not happen overnight. As many as were cheering the election of the new President, there were still 52 million people who did not share the collective winning view. For these 52 million of our countrymen, the very idea of "that one" being their President was, and still is, too repulsive an idea for them to stomach. For them, the slogan, "Change, Yes We Can," has been replaced with "Change, No We Won't."

Why? For some, the idea of change is something to be hated. Rather than change, they will protest, stand in utter opposition, and spread unfounded rumors to slow the growing movement. Then, if all else fails, they will rebel. Now, before we judge the opponents of change too harshly, the truth is, most of us are far more comfortable talking about other folks changing than we are about changing ourselves. When the real change being discussed requires an internal adjustment, such as changing our attitudes, our behavior, and/or giving up our long standing traditions, I am certain that we, too, would quickly adjust the slogan from "Change, Yes WE Can" to, "Change, Yes THEY Can."

Like it or not, the fundamental truth is, if you are a child of God, you must change. If we are to ever reach the heights that God has set for us, we all must change. Yes, change! I recognize that change can be a very daunting process, because real change must start from within. But, as children of the Most High God, if we believe that the Holy Spirit has been given to us to empower, nurture, comfort, convict, and teach us, then we should recognize that the Holy Spirit has been given to us to "c-h-a-n-g-e" us!

It is the Holy Spirit who will change us from what we are to what we can be. It is the Holy Spirit who will change us from being tied to the world to being tied to Christ. It is the Holy Spirit who will change us from being self-centered to self-sacrificing, from trouble makers to peace makers, from unfaithful to faithful, and from hateful to loving. Whether we choose to recognize and operate in the power of the Holy Spirit, the fact still remains that we have the Holy Spirit dwelling on the inside of us and, thus, have been given the power we need to change. The change that is to be accomplished in us is necessary in order to fulfill the will of God. This change is what enables us to use the life we have been given to not fulfill our own interests and desires, but to do the work of Him who has sent us, while it is day.

Consider Paul's instructions in Romans 12:2, "And be not conformed to this world: but be ye *transformed by the renewing of your mind, that ye may prove what is that good, and acceptable, and perfect will of God."* The urge and lust to do what is opposite of God's will for us can only be tempered by allowing the Holy Spirit to do the arduous work of change. This work is the only kind of work that sets us up to be able to navigate the vicissitudes of life.

Life's twists and turns come without warning, and can bring with them an unrelenting wave of emotions that, at times, become too intense to process. For example, a routine check-up at the doctor's office that ends with a cancer diagnosis or an undetermined amount of time to live. This is what I call a game changer. It would be the knock at the door that brings notification of a spouse' death and the realization he/she will never hear the words, "I'm sorry." Listening to the obstetrician as she repeats the news about the baby and the tangled cord, and then processing the reality that you're going to go through an emergency delivery... that is a game changer.

No matter how devastating the realities that life brings, it is only when we have allowed the Holy Spirit to do the sometimes painstaking work of change that our faith becomes fortified and our strength solidified. Paul put it perfectly, *"but though our outward man perish, yet the inward man is renewed day by day. For our light affliction, which is but for a moment, worketh for us a far more exceeding and eternal weight of glory"* (2 Corinthians 4:16-17). The type of change I am talking about is transforming change. This type of change is not an ordinary or simplistic change, but a metamorphosis that consists of a radical, mind blowing, and life altering change.

Believe me, there is nothing gentle, safe, or cut about a metamorphosis. The process can be grueling, laborious, and even strenuous, but the final result of the refiner's fire is a beauty that cannot be compared to the former self.

In Genesis 38:1-29, the biblical text gives a glimpse into the life of Tamar, a woman who experienced a game changing life experience, but was able to navigate these unexpected changes in her life in such a way that her actions were counted as righteous. She was able to accomplish this because she understood her position as well as the provision and the promises of God.

The Bible tells us that she was married to Jacob's son Er. However, due to Er's wickedness, God killed him. This was a game changer, because as a widow, Tamar could have been left wanting for food and shelter, wandering the wilderness to fend for herself. She was then given to Jacob's next eldest son, Onan. This was done in order that she might give birth to an heir, through whom she would have access to the inheritance that was rightfully hers.

To understand this inheritance ordained by God, it is important to examine her position with God. A position, albeit shared by all, I believe is especially established with women. As noted in the creation story of Genesis 2:7, 21-22, God created man from the dust of the earth. However, I believe, to illustrate God's special bond and love for women, God didn't reach back down to the earth and pick up more dust with which to form Eve, but God put Adam to sleep and formed Eve from Adam's rib. The Bible does not state how long Adam was under the

could rest, knowing that inherent in God's love was a promise not to be forgotten, and a provision that she would be taken care of. Tamar knew that, despite what it looked like, God had already begun to work and she could rest and move in God's appointed time. She could rest comfortably, because she knew that God put into biblical law, in Deuteronomy 25:5-10, a practice that would guarantee a woman in this situation an inheritance. The law stated, if the husband should die before he had an heir, his closest male relative would help his wife to conceive a child and when that child was born, the baby would be the dead man's heir. I would call this the 'Surrogate Provision.' Under this provision, all of the father's wealth would pass to his child, and thus, Tamar would keep all that she had because she would be the child's caretaker.

Onan understood this perfectly, but he had no intention of doing right by Tamar. He just wanted to get the pleasure without providing the provision. We are well acquainted with this type of individual. People like Onan are the ones who want all the fringe benefits without any of the documentation. Onan did not want to get Tamar pregnant because as long as his dead brother did not have an heir then at the time of his father's death, the double portion that would have rightfully gone to his brother's heir would go to him. In other words, he was an inheritance stealer!

Have you ever been victimized by an inheritance stealer? They are the ones who enter the lives of others with disingenuous motives, presenting themselves as one thing while attempting to keep God's promises and provisions from ever being obtained. An inheritance stealer is a brother who is envious of the love he sees between you and your fiancé, and, subsequently, extends his hand in friendship, only to see if he can keep the two of you from coming together. An inheritance stealer is the sister who recognizes your genius, and offers financing and a partnership with the intention of making off with your ideas. An inheritance stealer is that oh-so-subtle seducer, or seductress, called temptation, who whittles away at your ethics, siphons your integrity, and compromises your morality.

Part of the reason so many fall and succumb to inheritance stealers is because we do not trust God beyond what our eyes can see at the moment. Some of us are so fearful of the idea of change and transformation, even though we know it must take place, we would rather live beneath our privileges instead of trust God, who is willing and able to provide everything we will ever need. Some of us stay in abusive relationships, stay in abusive churches, stay under abusive pastors, and stay under abusive bosses, because we fear the unknown. Today, however, change is coming. Just as God moved Onan out of Tamar's life, He will in time move all of the people and all of the obstacles that are keeping you from the provisions He has promised you!

When Onan spilled his seed on the ground to prevent Tamar from getting pregnant, he was denying Tamar the inheritance, the provision that was ordained by God for her to have. So, God removed him. Now, God is coming after anyone and anything in your life that is blocking you from receiving what God has already ordained to be yours! Cold, nasty, indifferent, backbiting and backstabbing people – gone! Two-faced, arrogant, egomaniacal, power-hungry, condescending people – gone! Unfair policies and underhanded practices – over! Backroom politics and sidebar conferences – over! God's message to you is, stop worrying about having an Onan to provide for you, because God is the giver of your inheritance and the source of your provision.

In the text, after God removed Onan, Judah began to look at Tamar as if she were a black widow spider. He was afraid that if he gave Tamar his youngest son, Shelah, then he too would die. So, instead of giving Shelah to her right away, Judah told Tamar to go home to her parents and when Shelah was grown, he would give her to him as his wife. Judah told Tamar to go home and wait. Now, at this point, Tamar could have given up and allowed this situation to cripple her and make her resentful towards God and her present condition. But, rather than brood about the changes that continued to take place, she decided to hold on to God's unchanging hand and wait on God's time to move.

Now, this is where most of us get in trouble. We have the hardest time waiting on God. The text did not say Tamar grew impatient or bitter while she waited. She did not get ornery and start causing confusion. The reason she could rest and wait was she understood her position in God. When you understand your position in God, you can wait for the appointed time and then move with the calm assurance that God is going to work everything out for your good. You have to have the mindset of Job, who declared, *"All the days of my appointed time will I wait, till my change come"* (Job 14:14).

Many Christians need to take a lesson from Tamar and stop trying to help God. Just wait on God! Too many of us are running around like chickens with our heads cut off because we do not know how to wait. Too many of us are acting outside of what God wants us to do. Evidence of us moving outside of the will of God is having everything we touch fail. Instead of running around, we need to be still, seek God and ask Him to help us be righteous in our waiting. Ask God, "Am I honoring you with my time and service, or am I moving out of my own frustrations and desires?" The truth is that we have to wait, we must wait. It is in the waiting, in the incubator of time, that God is preparing us to handle the blessings that he is about to give us. However, if we do not do the hard task of being still, then we run the risk of pre-empting our own success and giving birth prematurely.

Now, at first glance, it looks like Tamar got tired of waiting and took matters into her own hands, but we must look again. Tamar was entitled by God's law to have Shelah, and in the absence of Shelah, she was entitled by the law to have another male blood relative. So, that meant Judah. Judah was obligated by law to give her an inheritance. Tamar waited on the appointed time. We know that it was ordained of God because, in the end, her action was counted as righteous. She did not go outside of the law. Judah declares, she was more righteous than he was in the sight of God! In addition, the provision and promise that God ordained was made manifest by the giving of life in her womb. There is only one right way, God's way.

We must come to the point in our lives where we stop looking for the back door, the short cut, and the loop hole. We must get to the point where we endeavor to simply do what God has commanded. For when we do, the breakthrough is coming. God will impregnate you with destiny, infuse you with purpose, and ignite you with power. No one will be able to take it from you, because it is your inheritance, you have a God-given right to possess it. It is God's gift to you for your faithfulness during your wait.

Nevertheless, you see, it is imperative that you do it God's way. If Tamar had truly played the harlot by deciding that she was going to have a baby by any old Joe, she would have lost her life, being stoned for adultery, which would've been authorized by the same law that entitled her to the inheritance and protection. When anyone steps outside of the will of God, they run the risk of losing their life. There are too many headlines about pastors, ministers, and children of God being jailed and investigated because they stepped outside of God's will. Too many stories of lives forever changed because of one bad decision to forsake God's command and fulfill our own lusts. However, when you wait on God, and do it His way, you will be under his protection because you will possess His signet and his rod!

During biblical times, the signet ring was a way of determining ownership. When heated by fire, the seal, or mark, made by the ring would designate ownership. This is good news, because once you and I accepted the Lord Jesus Christ as our Savior,

His signet ring, His mark, and His stamp was placed on us. So, we have become set apart for Him and by Him. At that moment, we were inducted into a royal priesthood and became joint heirs with Christ. Therefore, because we belong to God, our fellowship comes with position, provision, and promises! Ephesians 1:13 and 14 says we are *"stamped with the seal of the long promised Holy Spirit and that Spirit is the guarantee of our inheritance!"*

We also possess His staff, which should comfort our heart and mind during times of game changing transitions. It should comfort us because God is the eternal Good Shepherd, who is forever caring for His flock. The staff is not only used to guide and lead the flock, but is also used to defend and protect the flock.

For a long time, it seemed like Tamar had been forgotten and left without an inheritance, but God did not forget her, just as He has not forgotten us. God saw fit that Tamar's inheritance would come forth at the appointed time, and when it came, it was more than she ever anticipated. Likewise, with us, the blessing God will bestow upon us, at the appointed time, will be multiplied because of our faithfulness. Faithfulness notwithstanding, in order for the blessings to manifest itself in our lives, we must breakthrough our self-constructed mental cocoons.

Many of us are familiar with the story of the ugly caterpillar that enters into a cocoon and begins to undergo a metamorphosis that results in the caterpillar changing into a beautiful butterfly. I am told that each part of the process is necessary, especially the process at the end where the butterfly must struggle to get out of the cocoon. It is through that final process of struggling and wiggling and maneuvering to get out of the cocoon that the butterfly's wings receive and gain the strength they need to enable the new butterfly to soar.

If we are faithful to what God has ordained for us to do, God will, at the appointed time, bring forth the blessing, and no obstacle will be able to block it. We see in the text, in verse 27, that when it came time for Tamar to deliver, she had twins in her womb. A hand of one baby came out first and they marked it with a scarlet ribbon. That baby's hand, however, went back in. It was, then, the baby that was in the second position who came out first! So, they named the firstborn of the twins Perez, which means "breakthrough." For those of us who have been in the second position all of our lives, overlooked and forgotten, God is about to give you power to BREAKTHROUGH!

The blessing of being in the incubation chamber of the Holy Spirit, and having undergone the radical metamorphosis required to handle the blessing God is going to give, is, when the appointed time comes, you will come forth with POWER! You will have the power to repel the inheritance stealer, the power to dismiss the shame of your past, and the power to breakthrough any obstacle standing in your way. *"Now thanks be unto God, which always causeth us to triumph in Christ,"* (2 Corinthians 2:14). When God's favor comes upon you, no devil in hell, no fake friend, no jealous or envious brother or sister, and no past disappointment can keep it from you!

Lastly, just like with Perez, some of you think that your destiny is in the first blessing that God gave to you, but the real blessing is still in your womb. Your entire struggle and heart ache, was just the preparation you needed to strengthen your wings so you can ascend. Now it is time for you to do something. This declaration is backed by the words in James 2:20, *"Faith without works is dead."* It is time for you to push out the blessing that God has put inside of you. What good would it have done for God to put a double blessing in Tamar, if she never pushed them out? Perez is coming! The breakthrough is now, but you must push through the sadness, push through the pain, push through the disappointment, and push beyond the fatigue, in order to receive the inheritance that is promised!

In short, as children of the Most High God, we must undergo the arduous work of change. Yes, it is difficult, but it is also unavoidable. It is essential that this toiling process take place, so that we may be able to cast aside the urgings and cravings within us, that are contrary to the will and purpose ordained for us by God. Do not be fooled into thinking that this type of metamorphic change can be accomplished on our own. No! We are not capable. This kind of change is only achieved through the magnanimous power of the Holy Spirit working through us. This is the only way to bring about REAL change. Should we refuse to allow the Holy Spirit to do the work, we will not be able to withstand or survive the 'game changers' that plague us during this lifetime. Instead, we will continue to be susceptible to 'inheritance stealers,' and other paralyzing predicaments that cause us to implode and die.

On the other hand, when we recognize our position in God, then we can rest, as Tamar did, in the reassuring love of God and know that, at the appointed time, God will provide the promised provision. It is because our faith did not falter while we waited, that now the manifestation of God's bountiful blessing will be multiplied. As it says in Galatians 6:9, *"Be not weary in well doing for we shall reap in due season if we faint not!"* Moreover, we will have the power to breakthrough any barrier that tries to block our blessings.

"Unshackled from Rejection"

A sermon by JASMINE W. SCULARK

Genesis 21:1-21 (New Living Translation)

" *The Lord kept his word and did for Sarah exactly what he had promised. She became pregnant, and she gave birth to a son for Abraham in his old age . This happened at just the time God had said it would. And Abraham named their son Isaac. Eight days after Isaac was born, Abraham circumcised him as God had commanded. Abraham was 100 years old when Isaac was born. And Sarah declared, "God has brought me laughter. All who hear about this will laugh with me. Who would have said to Abraham that Sarah would nurse a baby? Yet I have given Abraham a son in his old age!" When Isaac grew up and was about to be weaned, Abraham prepared a huge feast to celebrate the occasion. But Sarah saw Ishmael—the son of Abraham and her Egyptian servant Hagar—making fun of her son, Isaac. So she turned to Abraham and demanded, "Get rid of that slave woman and her son. He is not going to share the inheritance with my son, Isaac. I won't have it!" This upset Abraham very much because Ishmael was his son. But God told Abraham, "Do not be upset over the boy and your servant. Do whatever Sarah tells you, for Isaac is the son through whom your descendants will be counted. But I will also make a nation of the descendants of Hagar's son because he is your son, too." So Abraham got up early the next morning, prepared food and a container of water, and strapped them on Hagar's shoulders. Then he sent her away with their son, and she wandered aimlessly in the wilderness of Beersheba. When the water was gone, she put the boy in the shade of a bush. Then she went and sat down by herself about a hundred yards away. "I don't want to watch the boy die," she said, as she burst into tears. But God heard the boy crying, and the angel of God called to Hagar from heaven, "Hagar, what's wrong? Do not be afraid! God has heard the boy crying as he lies there. Go to him and comfort him, for I will make a great nation from his descendants." Then God opened Hagar's eyes, and she saw a well full of water. She quickly filled her water container and gave the boy a drink. And God was with the boy as he grew up in the wilderness. He became a skillful archer, and he settled in the wilderness of Paran. His mother arranged for him to marry a woman from the land of Egypt.*

If I were to take a poll, I'm sure I would not be the only one who has ever felt the pain of rejection. While no one wants to experience rejection, we all have in some form or fashion. You may recall a childhood song about *Little Sally Walker*. It went something like this: "Little Sally Walker sitting in a saucer. Rise, Sally, rise; wipe your weeping eyes. Put your hands on your hip, and let your backbone slip. Oh, shake it to the east, shake it to the west, and shake it to the one that you love the best." If you were in another neighborhood, there was a second verse, "Your mama said so. Your papa said so." To those of you who are familiar with that song, and to those who are hearing it for the first time, have you ever wondered why Sally was sitting in a saucer? Why was Little Sally Walker depressed or down? Why was Sally crying? Sally was crying because Sally had experienced rejection. She had become an outcast.

Rejection means to be cast aside, outcast. Rejection means to be thrown away, as if you have no value. To be rejected is to be told, "I don't want you, and you don't have any value to me." Rejection, or being outcast or cast aside, means you are not what I want. You are not what is needed. Rejection is saying, "There is something about you that is not right."

Rejection is one of the key masterpieces of satanic oppression. Rejection is also the most untreated illness within the body of Christ. Whenever a person experiences rejection of any form, and on any stage, they tend to build up walls. Rejection does not stand alone, for it is a combination of abuse, guilt, and problems of identity and image. Rejection, or being an outcast, hinders the believer from ever experiencing full love, peace, joy and grace. Rejection is a collection of chains that has wrapped itself around us from something that has happened to us in the past.

Some of us have experienced rejection, not just as a child, but as an adult. Rejection may have come about because of the untimely death of a loved one. He/she may have been the one you thought would grow old with you. You assumed that your child would be burying you, but it turned out that you buried your child, and you feel a sense of rejection. As a child, some of you were left alone so often that now, somewhere in your mind and your spirit, you seem to be only content when you are away from everyone else. Maybe a parent left you with a terrible scar from the many times they told you that you were never going to be anything, that you were dumb, or that you were stupid.

Maybe, as a young child, you were touched by someone in an area where you should not have been touched. So, now as an adult, you are afraid to allow anyone to really touch you, because you can still feel that vile or nasty touch. Some have experienced rejection in a friendship, or a relationship. That rejection may have come in the form of a divorce, not physically, but an emotional divorce, living together but worlds apart.

Someone said that the greatest forms of rejection are from a parent, a child, or a divorce. A divorce speaks volumes to you and tells you that you are not wanted. After you have given your all to that person, revealed all of your strengths and weaknesses, and given them everything you have, they turn around and decide they don't want you anymore. They want someone else. Now, after so many years of a relationship, after the vow of forever, someone else is sitting in the car you bought, living in the house you decorated, or sleeping in the bed you made, you have concluded that because you have been rejected, you will never trust nor love again.

For some of us, you have experienced rejection because of the way you look, and ever since that day, you have been trying to look like everyone else.

When you experience any one of those events or moments, as a child or an adult, you subconsciously position yourself into three main areas: first, to be abused over and over, or, in turn, to become the abuser of others or yourself. You may begin receiving, what is called, self-inflicted wounds. For some young person to bear the burden of rejection from a parent, a boyfriend, or a girlfriend, and express that pain in an outward way by taking a sharp object and subjecting him/herself to bodily harm, this is what the world calls a "cutter." You don't want to die. You just want to punish yourself outwardly in a vain attempt to soothe the inward pain.

For others, you may have experienced some form of rejection, not because of how you look, but because of your sexuality. Maybe your parents and other members of your family have cast you away emotionally because of your sexual preference. For some, the rejection did not take place in the privacy of your own home but it was on the job. We live with it everyday, where people judge us, not by the content of our character, but by the color of our skin. Then we enter the four walls of the church, seeking safety, but experiencing more rejection. People talk around you, seeking to dehumanize you; causing others to misinterpret you.

The emotions tied to rejection and feeling like an outcast result in some of the most painful emotional wounds any human being can experience. Then, your emotions keep the pain fresh, as if you remember the pain as if it happened yesterday. You remember when you experienced being rejected, cast out, and cast aside. You also remember when you, in turn, ministered rejection to someone else.

Rejection has two sides. It has the side of the one who caused the rejection and the side of the one experiencing the rejection. The person causing it and the person experiencing it are both victims. If God can heal the person who has experienced painful rejection, surely God can heal the person who causes it.

You and I are not the first to experience rejection or being an outcast. Our biblical text introduces us to a parent, as well as a child, who both had a similar experience. Would you journey with me, as we examine the plight of this mother and son, and see what we can learn from their experience? Through their lives, we may be able to gain insight into how we, too, can become unshackled from rejection.

Let me say, at the very beginning, how it amazes me that the story of a person experiencing rejection or being cast out is found in the book of Genesis, which is the book of beginnings. It is suggesting to you and me that we are not the first, nor the last, to experience any form of rejection. Remember, the Bible says, "There is nothing new under the sun."

In our text we are introduced to a couple, with whom most of us should be very familiar, especially if you have been in the church for any significant amount of time. Even if you haven't, you may still know something about them. Not to mention that most of us have sung the childhood song which recites, "Father Abraham had many sons, had many sons, our father Abraham. I am one of them and so are you."

Now, let's go over some basic information about this couple. Abraham was married to Sarah. The Lord made a promise to Abraham and Sarah that they would have a child in their old age, and the child would be the promised one, the one through whom God would bless Abraham and Sarah for generations to come. As time crept along, Sarah grew impatient with God. After all, one year, five years, and then ten years had gone by, and Abraham and Sarah were not getting any younger. In fact, they were well up in age. In her haste, Sarah decided to take matters into her own hands. She suggested to Abraham that, because God was taking so long to fulfill his promise, maybe she and Abraham should just help God out. She gave Abraham her Egyptian handmaid, Hagar, and commanded him to have sex with her in order to produce the "promised seed." The account of that story can be found in Genesis 16.

Abraham honors the request of his wife and goes in to Hagar and they produce a child and name him Ishmael. Ishmael represents in scripture, the one that God allowed. He is known as the permitted one. Fourteen years later (Genesis 16:16; Genesis 21:5), Abraham and Sarah did have a child and named him Isaac. While Ishmael represents the permitted will of God, Isaac represents the perfect will of God.

In Abraham household, there were now two sons, Ishmael and Isaac, the permitted and the perfect will of God. One was the result of man's impatient attempt at creating God's plan, the other was the culmination of God's perfect plan. How well this demonstrates that, while God may not always come when you think he should, he is always on time.

We can see, through this situation, how some of things that happen in our lives are not the perfect will of God but they were permitted by Him. He allows these things to happen because, while He is all powerful, He will not interrupt man's free will. You and I have free will, which means, God will not force you to do anything you don't want to do. He tells us that if we don't praise him, it's on us, but the very rocks will cry out in our place. He won't force you to do anything you do not want to do, but he does set before you an open door. On either side of the door, there are consequences. The decision to go through the door will always be up to you. It's like what my mother always said, "You can lead a horse to the water, but you can't force him to drink." All I can do is offer you Bible study and ministry opportunities, but I cannot force you to come. Remember, with every decision there are consequences.

God is not out to punish you, but there are natural, as well as spiritual, consequences to every action. If you sell drugs and get caught, you will have to serve time. That is not God punishing you. It is the natural consequence for your actions. The Bible says, "Whatsoever a man sows that shall he also reap." If you have sex and do not use protection, then you find out that you got pregnant or contracted an infection; this is not God judging you because you chose to fornicate, it is the natural consequence of the decision you made. Whatever you sow is what you are going to reap. What goes around will come around. What goes up must come down. These are all natural principles.

The Bible said the rain falls on the just as well as the unjust. In other words, just because you are in church and love the Lord does not mean you are exempt from the consequences of your actions. The only difference is that a child of God has a grace factor. Paul tells us that just because you have grace, it does not mean you should abuse the grace. Grace is God giving you what you don't deserve, and mercy is God holding back what you do deserve.

We see the permitted and perfect will of God in our text, and for some of us, that's where we are. We are living in the permitted will and not the perfect will. We married this person, and got pregnant. Now, life is a little bit harder and we wonder why God is doing this to us. That's not God, that's the consequence of a wrong choice, a bad decision. Abraham and Sarah made a decision, and they had to live with the decision they made. Many of us know what it's like, living with a bad decision, the wrong choice, wishing you could roll back the hands of time, but you can't. All you have to do is pray, like the old people taught us to pray. "Lord, grant me the serenity to accept the things I cannot change, courage to change the things that I can…"

The Bible shows us that, after fourteen years of living with the permitted will of God, Sarah finally gave birth to the promise. The permitted did not stop

God's perfect will. Life was a little bit harder. The permitted slowed down the progress of receiving the perfect will, but it did not stop the promise. In the theological world, both boys represented a typology. Ishmael is the sin of the flesh. Isaac is the promise of the Spirit. The Bible says, "Both boys grew side by side." On one occasion, Sarah decided to have a birthday party for Isaac. The Bible tells us they were celebrating his birthday when, his mother, Sarah, saw Ishmael, the permitted one, laughing at her promised one, and she said, "Oh no!" So, she told Abraham in verse 10, "cast out this bondwoman and her son for the bondwoman and her son will not be heir with my son." In other words, "Abraham, get rid of them, cast them aside, and throw them out. I don't want them, and they have no value to us. We don't need her or her child anymore, we have our promise now."[16]

Now, when I first read this text, I thought Sarah was being a little hard and overly protective of Isaac. After all, it seemed like these boys were just being boys. But, when you really do some research, you find out that there is more to it. Something deeper lies beneath. Ishmael was fourteen years older than Isaac. When children are raised together, the elder should be careful and tender with the younger, but it argues a very basic and sordid disposition in Ishmael, for him to be abusive to a child who would, in no way, be able to physically contend with him.

Abraham was grieved and yet he honored Sarah's request. The next day Abraham woke up early and took bread and a bottle of water. I call that child support. He then places on the shoulders of Hagar, the burden of raising their son all by herself. The Bible says she departed and wandered in the wilderness, or wild-ness, of Beersheba. That's where rejection leads you: to a wandering state, in a wilderness. A place where you are asking yourself, over and over again, why? What did I do wrong? Neither Hagar nor Ishmael are to blame in this situation. That's the first word I want to say to those of you who have experienced rejection. Don't assume that the rejection you experience was because of something you've done. Sometimes it's about you, but, most of the time, it's not.

Rejection makes you wonder, was I not good enough. Rejection gets to the core of your self image, for it tells you that you are not valued. Rejection tells you that you are worthless. In fact, it tells you that you are only worth a piece of bread and a bottle of water. Some of us, because of childhood rejection, as well as rejection as adults, are wandering in the wilderness. We are wandering from one relationship to another, from one job to another, from one drug to another, from one church to another. We are wanderers. Our souls have no anchor. For some of us, we end up like Hagar: wandering all of our lives, asking, "Why me? Or what did I do wrong? Why did my mother or father give me up for an adoption? Why did my marriage end in a divorce?" Some of us are no longer wandering in the wilderness, we're dying in the wilderness.

Wilderness also stands for wild-ness. This is why some of you, at 14, have already had as many sexual partners as an adult at 30. At 18, you were on your second or third child. At 25, you had already contracted an infection. At 30, you've had two abortions. You are wandering in the wilderness. All out of bread and water, you have lost the essence of who you are.

There are three areas of wilderness, or three different circles, to which rejection can make you hostage. The first circle is insecurity. In this circle, you never find satisfaction. You begin to speak negative things that become reality. You say things like, everyone is better than you. You compare yourself to everyone. You are in a relationship where the other person has to know your every move, because they are insecure, and their insecurity can be a sign of rejection.

The second circle or area of wilderness is intimidation. In this circle, you are uncomfortable with success and the compliments of others. In this area, it seems that getting ahead or getting the attention makes you uncomfortable.

Then, beyond the circle of insecurity and intimidation, is the circle of isolation. In this circle you are more comfortable when you are alone, because you have built up layer upon layer of falsity. You have hidden yourself under layers of insulation. You've built walls behind walls and no one can get in! Before anyone can truly love you, the walls have to come down.

As we examine the text further we see that, when the water ran out and the bread was all gone, Hagar cast her child under one of the shrubs. Okay, you guys missed it. In Verse 10, Sarah told Abraham to cast her out, rejected her. As she is wandering in the wilderness, she, in return, cast her own flesh and blood out. She cast him under a tree. She cast him into a foster home. She cast him into an unhealthy environment, because she is repeating what she knows and has experienced. Most people who reject or devalue another human being do so because they have been rejected or devalued. Now, again, Ishmael, the child, did nothing wrong. He is the only innocent person in this entire sordid fiasco. He is suffering because of the decisions made by the adults in his life.

I want to say to the young persons who have been blaming yourself for your parents' divorce, and your parents' issues, because you think that Mom or Dad are not just rejecting each other, but they are rejecting you. While they tell you over and over again, "this is not about you. It's just between mommy and daddy." Somehow, you think if you were a better child, it wouldn't end like this. You are caught in the crossfire, you are an innocent bystander.

According to the Bible, the person who has been cast out now becomes the one who casts their own family out. Hagar did not think she had what it took to keep her son alive, and she did not want to see him die. I wish I could talk to many of you who have been adopted. Those of you who think you were put up for adoption because your mother did not love you. You were put up for adopted because she *did* love you, she just did not believe she had what it took to keep you alive and she did not want you to die.

I know that Hagar did not want to cast Ishmael aside because the Bible said she lifted up her voice and wept. The text said, "And the Lord heard the voice of the lad."[17] This means that while she is crying, Ishmael is lifting up his voice. You know what that means young people? You can intercede on behalf of your parents. God not only heard the voice of the Ishmael, but God dispatched an angel to minister to his mother.

The angel asked her what was wrong. Now, you do know that God knows what's wrong? I know that to be a fact, because he does not even wait for her to answer! He says, "Fear not, for God has heard the voice of the lad. Arise, lift up the lad and hold him for I will make him a great nation."[18] God opened her eyes, and she saw a well of water and went and filled the bottle with water and gave her son a drink. They dwelled in the wilderness. Notice, he did not die, but he dwelled: became productive, became an archer. Ishmael became someone in the wilderness. Hagar and Ishmael became unshackled from their rejection. They did not allow what happened in their past to hinder their progress, nor kill their future.

The good news, for those who have experienced rejection: we can be unshackled from past and present forms of rejection.

How, then, do I become "Unshackled from Rejection?" How do I shake loose the wounds and scars and pain of rejection? Well, the text is tailored to teach us three things in this regard. First, and foremost, to become unshackled from rejection, you are going to need enough faith to rise above it. In verse 18, "Arise" means to get up.[19] Rejection can paralyze you in such a way that you go into a deep depression. You can wallow in self pity, feel like your world is out of control, and lose your strength, focus and joy of living. After all of this, the last thing on your mind is getting up. You would rather stay where you are. You are stuck in the situation or wilderness. You are going to have to develop the faith to rise. You have to move away from crying over things that you cannot do anything about. Notice that faith is active. You can, by faith, rise above that which is hanging over your head.

Second, you are going to have to learn to forgive. Notice, Hagar never went back. She learned to forgive. Forgiving is, sometimes, the hardest step. To forgive means to let it go. It carries the meaning of unmerited favor being given to the very person whom you feel doesn't deserve it. Forgiveness, however, is not about the other person. Forgiveness is about you. Something freeing happens to you when you extend unmerited favor to someone who has done wrong to you.

Now, I do say you have to learn to forgive. This means it will not come overnight. Forgiveness is the act of setting someone free from an obligation. For example, a debt is forgiven when you free your debtor of the obligation of paying back what he owes. Those people who have hurt you in the past, and who are hurting you now, will continue to do so unless you forgive them. You see, Abraham and Sarah had gone on with their lives. Hagar could not allow them to hinder her by carrying unforgiveness towards them. To forgive means we have to deal with the seven steps that happen to us when we have been hurt or have experienced rejection. The steps are as follows: First, there is the hurt; then, we become confused; we look for detours; we dig a hole; we deny it; we then become defeated and discouraged as the spirit of rejection gets a hold of us.

Finally, we must learn to make the best out of a bad situation. While what happened to Hagar and Ishmael was not the perfect will of God, they learned to make the very best out of the situation. What happened was not good, but God took all of it and worked it all together for their good.

Good things came out of this painful situation. Hagar got a vision for her life. The Bible said that her eyes were opened. Sometimes, it is in going through the wilderness that your eyes are opened. President Nixon said, after being pardoned by President Ford on Watergate, "Everyone calls you when you win, but only your friends call you when you fail." Sometimes, it has to be in the midst of a messed up situation for your eyes to be opened. You are able to see clearly your destiny and your purpose.

Notice, the text said, "The boy grew."[20] Rejection can also be a great tool for growth. In spite of the pain of rejection, Ishmael grew. We call this 'growing pains.' Would you like to know when you are most dangerous to the devil? It's when, in the midst of a mess, you are still growing and praising and seeking God. And may I remind you that, spiritual growth is not in the absence of trials and pain, but spiritual growth is in the midst of the mess. Would like to know what you are made of? It's not revealed when you are on the top of the mountain. It's revealed when you are in the valley, and in the lion's den. Anyone can praise God, sing a joyous song, and preach when all is going well. Anyone can talk about how they love you when all is going well.

It's another thing to be able to do all of this when mess is happening all around you.

May I remind you, in the book of Acts, the church's biggest growth came under trials and persecution? The Bible says, over and over again in the book of Acts, *"And the church was persecuted but the church grew."*[21] The reason why they grew brings me to another positive thing that happened to Hagar and Ishmael. The text said, "The lad grew because God was with him, and he became an archer." He became productive and not destructive. He found his purpose, and his destiny. It said, *"The Lord was with him and he dwelled."*[22] He didn't die, but he dwelled.

In other words, he became "Unshackled from Rejection" for production. You cannot be productive until you are willing to let go of rejection. You cannot be productive until you let go of trying to be destructive. In the midst of all of that, the text says, "And his mother took him a wife from Egypt."[23] He was free to love and be loved.

My beloved brothers and sisters don't allow rejection to steal away from you the greatest opportunity God has extended to us, which is to love and be loved.

"A Window of Opportunity"

A sermon by GINA M. STEWART

Mark 14:1-9 (International Standard Version)

"It was now two days before Passover and the Festival of Unleavened Bread. The leading priests and the teachers of religious law were still looking for an opportunity to capture Jesus secretly and kill him. "But not during the Passover celebration," they agreed, "or the people may riot. " Meanwhile, Jesus was in Bethany at the home of Simon, a man who had previously had leprosy. While he was eating, a woman came in with a beautiful alabaster jar of expensive perfume made from essence of nard. She broke open the jar and poured the perfume over his head. Some of those at the table were indignant ."Why waste such expensive perfume?" they asked. "It could have been sold for a year's wages and the money given to the poor!" So they scolded her harshly. But Jesus replied, "Leave her alone. Why criticize her for doing such a good thing to me? You will always have the poor among you, and you can help *them whenever you want to. But you will not always have me. She has done what she could and has anointed my body for burial ahead of time. I tell you the truth, wherever the Good News is preached throughout the world, this woman's deed will be remembered and discussed."*

"It's not the critic who counts, not the man who points out how the strong man stumbled, or when the doer of deeds could have done better. The credit belongs to the man who is actually in the arena; whose face is marred by dust and sweat and blood; who strives valiantly; who errs and comes short again and again; who knows the great enthusiasms, the great devotions and spends himself in a worthy cause; who, at the best, knows, in the end, the triumph of high achievement; and who, at the worst, if he fails, at least fails while daring greatly, so that his place shall never be with those cold and timid souls who know neither victory nor defeat" (Theodore Roosevelt).

Roosevelt's words may be even more relevant today than when he spoke them in 1910. As much as we would like to "play it safe" and live life in a risk-free zone, these words serve as a reminder that, if we desire to live a life of impact, there will be times when our purpose and calling demand that we reject a tendency toward ambiguity and place our necks on the line for that in which we believe. We must dare to be different. Dr. Martin Luther King, Jr. once said, "In spite of the imperative demand to live differently, we have cultivated a mass mind and have moved from the extreme of rugged individualism to the even greater extreme of rugged collectivism. We are not makers of history, we are made by history.[24]" We are not called to do or be something that gains the world's approval. We must dare to take the initiative even if it means being misunderstood. We will see how both President Roosevelt's and Dr. King's words capture the spirit of the woman from the Biblical passage above.

It is two days before the Jewish feast of the Passover, and Jesus is journeying to Jerusalem in preparation for the Passover events that will take place there. At this point, the Pharisees and religious leaders are at attention, ready and waiting for the opportunity to arrest and kill him; which was precipitated by Jesus' raising Lazarus from the dead on the previous return to Bethany. The scriptures are leading up to descriptions of the final, extremely meaningful, events in the life and ministry of Jesus before his crucifixion. The men who have accompanied him from the early days will become increasingly doubtful and confused, misunderstanding him, his ministry, and his mission.

The disciples are already protesting at the mention of his death. They will soon have to fight the creeping in of hopelessness as they watch the Messiah, the Chosen One of God, endure torture, humiliation and death. We'll see the foolishness in the hearts of two disciples exposed, as they are willing to exchange their mission for prominent places of honor in the kingdom. Denied by one disciple, betrayed by another, and accused of rebellion and treason, Jesus will become an increasingly isolated figure, as most of his followers desert him in the moments surrounding his arrest. But, before he faces all of this, one of the most important acts of honor will take place.

Shortly before the events surrounding his arrest and crucifixion, Jesus stops again in Bethany and shares a meal at the home of Simon, who once suffered from leprosy. During this meal, an unnamed woman enters the room where Jesus and other men are dining. She carries with her an alabaster box full of precious perfumed oil, worth a year's wages. She breaks the jar that contains the perfume and pours the perfume on Jesus' head.

Needless to say, the woman's extravagant gesture attracted the anger and criticism of Jesus' male counterparts. They scolded the woman for wasting the perfume on Jesus rather than selling it and donating the money. I believe that it is safe to say, these men completely missed the symbolic significance of the woman's actions. This unnamed, anonymous woman did not wait for someone to give her permission to do what she did. She acted courageously, in obedience to God, even at the risk of being misunderstood.

Who was this woman? While the accounts given by Mark and Matthew (Mark 14:3; Matthew 26:7) give us no specifics, we do know from John's account (John 12:3) that the woman was Mary, sister of Lazarus, whom Jesus had raised from the dead. She may have been just a footnote to the story, but her actions created a fundamentally different situation. She was unashamed and unapologetic. This woman of no societal status, stepped in with boldness and compassion, and took a risk.

Mary didn't walk into the all male meeting with a hidden agenda to get acceptance from the men, or to try to impress them in any way. She walked, with purpose, into this all male gathering, because she was a woman on an assignment. She didn't stop her assignment to consider tradition and or to maintain proprieties. In fact, her actions went completely against the accepted manners and conventional customs of that time. This woman was willing to go to extraordinary lengths to minister to Jesus and she had no shame in making sure her assignment was carried out!

What would make this woman do such a thing? Especially in the culture and setting in which she ministered? If we look at this text a little closer, we will find that Mary must have been given prophetic insight and instinct for this moment. She saw clearly and knew, supernaturally, what to do because she knew to whom she was ministering.

Take notice, this woman doesn't just anoint Jesus in the same way that one would anoint a dead body, but she pours the precious ointment on Jesus' head. Yes, dead bodies were anointed as a sign of reverence and to assist in preservation, but, anointing served other purposes as well. A host would anoint his guests to refresh them, sick people were anointed for curing, and the chosen king was anointed by the prophet. By her actions, the woman breaks with ancient Israelite tradition, and in an indirect way, assumes the role of a prophet. Not the title of a prophet, but the role of a prophet.

In ancient Israel, the prophet anointed the one who had been chosen as the new king. At God's bidding, Samuel anointed Saul, and later David, as king, pouring a flask of oil on their heads. The very same ritual performed by the prophet Samuel for Saul and David is exactly what the woman does for

Jesus. While not a famous prophet, she assumes a prophetic role, operating in what Dr. Cheryl Sanders in her book, Ministry at the Margins, refers to as "a prophetic initiative and imperative." Dr. Sanders further states, in the book, "She demonstrated the courage of and initiative of a prophet. She is willing to speak for God with symbolic actions and she acted in obedience to God even when no one in the room understood or accepted her gestures of love."

She breaks the alabaster jar and anoints the head of Jesus with her perfume. Anointing the head belonged to the designation of kings. The woman's gesture is seen as a symbolic recognition of Jesus being the King of Israel. This woman knew that she was not just anointing what would soon be a dead body; she was anointing the head of the King. The Messianic secret was revealed to an unrespected woman before it was revealed to the disciples.

The woman, Mary, recognizing Jesus' Kingdom identity, was willing to do what the men sitting with Jesus wouldn't. Having received revelation from God, she didn't go on with life as usual and pretend to not know who Jesus was or what she was called to do. She also didn't wait for everyone else to catch the revelation before she acted on it. With no visible role models, supporters, or encouragement, she takes the initiative to serve Jesus. Even though no one else in the room recognized what she was doing, or why, she broke the jar, to anoint our King's head with her precious ointment.

There comes a time when, once we recognize who Jesus is, we can no longer be guided by imitation and impulse, and hindered by indecisiveness. When you understand who Jesus really is, you are willing to take risks and do things that others wouldn't readily do. You'll go places where others wouldn't dare go, raise issues that others wouldn't raise. You will be willing to test the limits and push the boundaries. This woman knew who Jesus was and acted prophetically, even though the culture would have defined her actions as inappropriate and out of order.

I'm going to let you know that when you decide to minister to Jesus in a manner that is fit for a king, you can expect some real opposition. There will always be those who will be suspicious of your actions. There will be accusers, critics, liars, and haters. Sometimes you will be criticized by those you would never expect. Other times you will be opposed by those that you would expect to support you. Break the jar anyway! The woman had critics who thought their argument seemed logical, but Jesus said they were wrong.

We see from John's recap of the story, that Judas verbally raised the question of "Why?"— *Why wasn't this perfume sold and the money given to the poor* (John 12:5)? He questions the woman's choice of sacrifice. Of course, now, we know his motives were impure; but it seems that he had the shared support of the other disciples in his disapproval of the woman's sacrifice (Matthew 26:8-9; Mark 14:4-5). They argued that her lavish gift was a waste, claiming that the funds could have been used to do better things, like helping the poor. Jesus helped them to see that while the opportunity to do ministry and helping the poor is always right, and always available, the opportunity to minister to him in this way, at this time, would not be available again.

Rather than criticizing the woman's actions, Jesus defends her sacrificial choice. He lets the disciples know that this was a window of opportunity, and she responded in a way that was pleasing to God. In verse 7 of John's rendition, Jesus states, "it was intended that she should use this perfume for this moment." This woman may have done many other good things in her life, but this moment, this opportunity taken, happened to be the only reason that she is known by virtually every believer. She did what she could when the window of opportunity opened. Every day, we have a window of opportunity to do a loving act in the name of Jesus, despite the cost, the condemnation, or the critique.

As you look at the opportunities before you, what is it that God intends for you to do? Like our sister in the text, we have a window of opportunity. Like Mother Teresa, who became God's light to the poor of Calcutta, we have a window of opportunity. Like Mother Clara Hale, who cared for needy children in Harlem, and like Osceola McCartney, who donated $150,000 of her own, hard-earned, money to students, we have a chance to take advantage of our windows of opportunity. These windows of opportunity can lead to living a life of power and purpose for the kingdom of God and acting under divine authority to do something significant for Jesus right now; not tomorrow, not next week, not next month, but right now.

Remember, there WILL be opposition! Opposition will always be there. You, however, must be like the woman with the alabaster box: face your opposition and do what you can for Jesus while you can. There will always be haters, liars, critics, naysayers, skeptics, and cynics, but don't miss your window of opportunity! The text makes it clear to us that when you take advantage of your window of opportunity, heaven will back you up. Jesus told the woman's critics to leave her alone. He's already done the same for you. God has already rebuked your devourer (Malachi 3:11) and given you the authority to condemn every tongue that rises against you in judgment (Isaiah 54:17). So, don't miss your chance to do something great for Jesus.

Windows of opportunity are limited. God has placed you where you are, with the chance to use your resources and do something significant for him at this moment. Honor him while you have the opportunity. We know that we can do it, because Jesus did it first. Thank God that, at Calvary, Jesus did something of cosmic significance, to save us! The Word of God reminds us that, at the "right time" Christ died for the ungodly. Hallelujah! Amen!

"Go In the Strength That You Have"

DR. BARBARA WILLIAMS-SKINNER

The Graduation Ceremony message delivered in Washington, DC to Nyack College.

Judges 6:11-16 (The Message)

"*One day the angel of God came and sat down under the [tree] that belonged to Joash the Abiezrite, whose son Gideon was threshing wheat in the winepress, out of sight of the Midianites. The angel of God appeared to him and said, "God is with you, O mighty warrior!" Gideon replied, "With me, my master? If God is with us, why has all this happened to us? Where are all the miracle-wonders our parents and grandparents told us about, telling us, 'Didn't God deliver us from Egypt?' The fact is, God has nothing to do with us—he has turned us over to Midian." But God faced him directly: "Go in the strength that is yours. Save Israel from Midian. Haven't I just sent you?" But Lord, Gideon asked, "how can I save Israel? My clan is the weakest in Manasseh, and I am the least in my family.*

189

*The LORD answered, "I will be with you, and you
will strike down all the Midianites together."*

There is a word in the sixth chapter of the Old
Testament Book of Judges for you who are seeking
the strength to engage and change a world that often
looks like it has more hate than harmony, more
meanness than mercy, more decadence than decency,
and more fear than faith. Here was Israel: a loose
confederacy of tribes living in Canaan, the land that
Joshua had conquered, the land which was promised
by God. Without the strong leadership of men like
Moses, Joshua, and Caleb, they repeatedly fell into
idolatry, foreign political domination, intermarriage
with pagans, and other sins. They were in a general
state of spiritual confusion.

Judges 17:6 describes this time in Israel's
history as a time when "every man did that which
was right in his own eyes." They called themselves
"God's people," but you really could not tell the
difference between them and the unbelievers in their
world. They became weakened, not only spiritually,
but also militarily, and were consistently terrorized
by the stronger, better organized Midianites, who
were descendants of Abraham and his African wife,
Keturah.

Worse, was that they were more content to
recall, rehearse, and recite the deeds of great leaders
before them than to do what these leaders did – obey
God in the good and tough times. They loved to recite
what God did through their ancestors: Abraham, with
great faith in the One he called Jehovah Jireh, forged

a personal covenant with God; Jacob, our model of real peacemaking through his reconciliation with Esau (the brother whose birthright Jacob stole), fathered the twelve tribes of Israel; Joseph, who forgave his brothers after being sold into slavery by them, overcame rejection, temptation, and oppression to become governor over Egypt; Moses, who led the Israelites out of Egypt, through the wilderness, and to the border of the promised land, witnessed God parting the Red Sea and personally received from God, the Ten Commandments that the Israelites were to follow; Joshua, great warrior leader, did not care what the committee said about the impossibility of overcoming enemies in the wilderness proudly proclaimed, "as for me and my house, we will serve the Lord."

They recited the courageous acts of these trailblazers in the same way that we recite the journeys and acts of the trailblazers in our history. It would be as familiar as retelling the stories of Sojourner Truth, Harriet Tubman, Frederick Douglass, Rosa Parks, Caesar Chavez, Mary McLeod Bethune, Martin Luther King Jr., or Coretta Scott King. They made their heroes larger than life and forgot they were ordinary people through whom God moved in extraordinary ways.

All the while, the Israelites forgot the commands of God and began compromising with the world. They failed to remember that God changed them so they could change the world—and attract people to Him. Soon, the only way to tell believers from non-believers was religious rituals, language, and events.

So, God turned them over to their enemies, the Midianites, for seven years.

Things got so bad, that the children of Israel were living in caves in the sides of the mountain in order to hide from the Midianites. The powerful Midianites would even wait for the Israelites to plant their crops, then, they would come in and take over their fields with livestock, until the resources were practically gone, bringing Israel to complete poverty. So, the children of Israel were forced to try and find sneaky ways to harvest grain to eat. That's where God called Gideon. Gideon was in a winepress, a deep pit in the ground, out of sight of the Midianites, threshing wheat.

Like we all do when our disobedience leads to disaster, the Israelites cried out to God. Then the angel of the Lord appeared to Gideon and said three amazing things to a people who were caught between changing the world and becoming like the world.

First, the angel of the Lord let Gideon know "God is with you" (verse 12). There are times in our lives, individually and as a people, when the calamities, challenges, and crises we face may overshadow our view of God and make Him look pale and puny. Times like these may cause us to wonder, "Where is God when you need Him?"

We even know, intellectually, that God Almighty stepped out on, seemingly, nothing and created everything; that HE IS, from everlasting to everlasting; that His ways are beyond our figuring out; and that He is the Great I AM. Still, with all of this intellectual knowledge of God, the questions arise:

where was God when terrorists blew up the World Trade Center, attacked the Pentagon, and unleashed a spirit of fear on America? Where was God during the last 25 years, when 25 million people died of HIV/AIDS—and we still have 40 million currently infected the AIDS virus, including 700,000 children? Where is God when, according to the Children's Defense Fund, every 36 seconds a child is born into poverty, every minute a baby is born to a teen mother, every eight minutes a child is arrested for violent crimes, every three hours a child or teen is killed with a gun, and every five hours a child or teen commits suicide? Where was God when 400,000, mostly poor and mostly African American citizens, were displaced by Hurricane Katrina, with many still struggling to get their lives back?

Here we are, over 40 years since Martin Luther King Jr. shared his dream for an inclusive America, and racial alienation, polarization, and hate crimes are on the increase. The world panders filth 24-7, day after day, on the air waves, totally robbing children of their innocence. We're in a sex obsessed society, which is weakening the nation's moral foundations. In times like these, the tendency of God's people is to do self-help: to move without God, and find ways to meet their own needs.

Abraham tried self-help when God did not show up quick enough to give him the son he promised. David tried self-help and ended up committing adultery and instigating murder against Bathsheba's husband. Jonah tried self-help and ended up in the belly of a large fish, distraught and suicidal. Another definition for self-help is sin.

Sin is not always about stealing, lying, or sleeping around. Sin is choosing to do my thing over God's thing. Sin is being led by our ego, which is said to be Edging God Out! When God doesn't show up fast enough, one may marry the wrong person. When God doesn't answer when and how one wants, one may make wrong decisions and end up defeated. After we fail with the self-help, then we cry out to God for spirit-led help.

Somehow, we forget that the earth is the Lord's. He made heaven and earth without you. He holds the world in the hollow of his hand. He knows everything there is to know about you and has numbered every hair on your head. He has carved your name into the palm of his hand and has ordained your destiny, not your defeat. If only you'd get to know Him for whom He is!

He's not your bellhop. But, He is the bridge to your future. He's not your waiter. But, He is the Watchman over your life. He's not your personal attendant. But, He is your personal God. You need to get to know Him for who and what He really is, your Savior.

Abraham called Him – Jehovah Jireh – My God who provides. David called Him – Jehovah Ro`i – My Shepherd. Moses called Him – Jehovah Nissi – My banner of love. Rahab called Him – the "God of heaven above and the earth beneath". Jehoshaphat found Him to be the All Breasty One who fights our battles – El Shaddai. Isaiah called Him – Wonderful Counselor, Mighty God, Everlasting Father, and the Prince of Peace. We know Him also as Jesus the

Christ, God in the flesh, who can do anything but fail!

When God says "I am with you," He means just that. While others have failed you, left you, disappointed you, lied on and sabotaged you, God is your never-leaving, ever-present Jehovah Shammah; your healing Jehovah Rapha; your sanctifying Jehovah Tsidkenu; and your peace Jehovah Shalom.

The second thing the angel of the Lord said to Gideon was, "Mighty Warrior." God called Gideon by a name that defined how God saw him; not how Gideon saw himself. One problem many of us have today, we define ourselves by the standards others have set for us, instead of by the destination God has designed for us.

God called Gideon "mighty warrior" as a testament that God saw him as having the strength of courage and character to meet the crises he would face ahead. That was far more than Gideon saw in himself. Gideon totally missed God's lofty view of him! He actually began to express to the angel of the Lord his distress at the many challenges his people were facing. Gideon complained that God was not blessing them to the magnitude that He blessed the ancestors who were brought out of Egypt and then out of the wilderness. Clearly, Gideon forgot that those who rebelled against God never made it out of the wilderness and into the land that was promised.

Then, Gideon did something that we, far too often, do ourselves: he reminded God of how weak and incapable he was. Gideon was selling himself short of what God had already called him, saying,

"My clan is the weakest in Manasseh, and I am the least in my family" (verse 15). How much time do we spend cancelling out what God has called us to do and to be? He says we can do all things through Christ, we say: I am a woman, who will listen to me; I am too Black, too Brown, too Asian, or too White; I am too old to start doing this now; I'm a 'no one', too unknown to answer God's call to lead my generation.

In today's times, while we selfishly question our qualifications, our families are falling apart; our children are insulting us in their music; our wars are never ending; our men of color are locked up in prisons and unprepared to live, or make a living, when they get out; and our globe is reeling under the HIV/Aids pandemic. We need to remember that God is looking, not for perfect people, but for principled, praying, faith-filled people, who are in love enough with Jesus Christ, who are angry enough about the moral decline of our nation, and who are outraged enough about the injustices of our world to want to do something about it!

I know that as believers, we often times wonder, "what can I do to save the world," or "what can I do to address the issues facing my generation… after all, I am only ONE person!" The fact is, all God has ever needed is one person!

One person, ABRAHAM, believed God enough that God established a covenant with the Israelites. That covenant now covers all who believe. One person, MOSES, despite personal limitations, was used by God in the liberation of an entire nation from Egyptian bondage. One person, DAVID, despite the adultery and murder on his resume, was called by God "a man after God's own heart" because he faced his fears, took ownership of his weaknesses, and answered the call of servant leadership. One person, DANIEL, in a national crisis abandoned everything and prayed until deliverance came. One person, ESTHER, forsook her grand position as a Persian beauty queen and stood in the gap to foil a plan of extermination against her Jewish people. One person, PETER, gave up his bigotry against the Gentiles to become a mighty spiritual warrior for God and the church. One person, PAUL, a fanatical serial killer of Christians, answered the call of God and became the author of most of the New Testament.

The power of one person didn't stop after the Bible was written. When national crisis and moral decline again threaten to consume God's people, we see ordinary men and women used by God in extraordinary ways, because they were available to Him. These men and women heard the same call that Gideon heard: "Mighty Warrior! GO IN THE STRENGTH THAT YOU HAVE."

William Wilberforce went in the strength that he had and helped to end the English slave trade. John Wesley answered the call to preach and teach the uncompromising gospel, while advocating the abolition of slavery. William Booth, an iterant street preacher in the slums of London, took up the cause of those Jesus called "the least of these," and in 1965 began the Salvation Army. William Seymour, the son of ex-slaves, turned a tiny horse stable on Azusa Street in Los Angeles into an internationally famous center of miracles and revival in the early 1900s. He brought together black and white Christians, for the first time, in a spirit of worship. C. S. Lewis, called the "apostle of skeptics," wrote, powerfully, about the Lordship of Jesus and attracted millions to Christ.

Dietrich Bonhoffer, a young German Pastor, left the safety of America, returned to Germany, repudiated the Nazis, and paid the cost of discipleship with his very life. Mother Theresa of Calcutta, whose Home for the Dying in Calcutta helped the poorest of the poor find dignity, even in facing death, demonstrated that God does not call us to be successful, He calls us to be faithful. Rosa Parks, seamstress and secretary of the Montgomery, Alabama NAACP, simply responded to her understanding of the fact that we are all created in the image and divinity of God, and refused to give up her seat to a white man, sparking a major push in the Civil Rights Movement. John Perkins, who was beaten nearly to death in a Mississippi jail for protesting segregation, has become a modern day prophet of racial and economic justice. Martin Luther King, Jr., who, in 1954, at age 25, took his new bride, Coretta Scott King and went to his first job as pastor of the Dexter Avenue Baptist Church in Montgomery, Alabama. King wanted only to be a family man like his father, Daddy King, raise his children, and preach the Gospel. Yet, he responded to God's call to "Go in the strength you have" and God used him mightily to transform our world by teaching the power of nonviolent resistance to oppression and bigotry.

The list is long of ordinary, everyday people, filled with the same fears, frailties, personal hopes, and dreams that you have. These are people who heard that same call that Gideon heard, *"Mighty*

Warrior," and the Words of Jesus, *"If you love me then keep my commandments."* These are the ones who believed what Jesus taught when he said, *"Why call me Lord, Lord and do not do what I tell you."* These people heard the teachings of Apostle Paul, *"HE who began a good work in [me], will perfect it until the day of our Lord, Jesus Christ."*

They remembered the Words of Jesus telling us, as he was preparing for his death on the cross, that even though we have seen him heal the sick, raise the dead, give sight to the blind, give hope to the disinherited, the left out, the least, and the last, there is still a message for us, *"greater works than these will you do, because I am going to my Father."* They knew, like the late Tom Skinner, former Harlem, New York gang leader turned evangelist and author of the best selling, "Black and Free," that Christian is spelled C-H-R-I-S-T-I-A-N. Meaning 'Christ in you,' living his life through you, without any help or assistance from you. All that's needed is just your availability!

To be a Christian means to be a follower of Jesus Christ. We must be a follower and not merely an observer. We must be a follower and not just a teacher. We must be a follower and not exclusively a preacher. If we are to be true followers of Christ, we must aspire to go beyond believing what Christ believes (the Bible says that even the Devil believes and tremble). Being a follower of Jesus Christ means, doing what Christ did!

Here, God is saying, 'I know the trouble you are in. I know the size and fortitude of your enemies, I know you are being terrorized from the outside, but I also know that some of your wounds are self-inflicted and come from the inside as a result of your compromised spiritual values. Compromises that include: talking holy, but living unholy; talking about justice, but not doing what is just.'

'Nevertheless, I heard your cry, and because I love you, I am with you. As I was with Abraham, Isaac, and Jacob, I am with you. I am Emmanuel. I am a personal God, and a redeeming God, who has chosen to be revealed in you. You, the one waiting, in great anticipation, to reach some milestone in your life before you'll believe that I have called you.'

That milestone is now. Never has there been a time when the need for committed, compassionate, courageous, Christ-minded servant leaders has ever been greater, nor has the crises of the times ever been more overwhelming. Your Midianites (your challenges) may be very different from Gideon's, but they are equally treacherous and deadly.

The third thing that God said to Gideon, which still speaks to us today, is, "Go in the strength that you have, and save Israel out of Midian's hand. Am I not sending you?" (Verse 15) When He has to address the problems of His nation, God will use seemingly weak people to do mighty things:

> → He used JACOB: a deceiver, fathered the Israelite nation
> → He used JOSEPH: a slave, saved his whole family
> → He used ESTHER: a slave girl, saved an entire race of people from massacre

→ He used MARY: a peasant teenage girl, became the mother of Christ

→ He used MATTHEW: a tax collector, became an apostle and Gospel writer

→ He used PETER: a fisherman and loud mouth, became an apostle, lead the early church, and wrote two New Testament letters.

So, Gideon went and organized an army of 22,000, which God whittled down to 300. With 300 men, chosen by God, facing thousands of Midianites... Gideon's army prevailed. Gideon learned in that moment, that with God on our side-our fear can become the pathway to our faith: "If God is for us, who can be against us?"; "The battle is not yours but the Lord's"; "Our enemies will come at us one way and flee seven ways"; "He who has begun a good work in you, will perfect it until the day of our Lord, Jesus Christ."

Today, God is saying to believers just what he said to Gideon, "Mighty Warriors, go in the strength you have and save your people?" With this charge, God gives us the instructions. First, He is calling you to be a messenger of reconciliation in a world where we talk diversity, but practice division. 2 Corinthians 5:17 says, *"If any person is in Christ Jesus, they are a new creation, the old has passed away the new has come, all this is from God who reconciled us to himself through Christ and gave us the ministry of reconciliation."*

God is calling some "mighty warriors" to rescue God's people from the faulty theology that says, "I am personally saved! I no longer commit the personal sins I used to commit, but I will keep on thinking and believing the same bigoted thoughts I used to think about others who are not like me." This just means, you're still the same person you were before God saved you, with an unregenerate mind and all!

We need some mighty warriors to help God's people understand that reconciliation is not about race, gender, or generational and religious divisions. The word reconciliation comes from the word *katallasso*, which means "an exchange." An exchange is what happened when we renounced our old lives and accepted the new life in Jesus Christ, the author of our salvation. Salvation is reconciliation, because we are reconciled to God, out of the alienation into which all humans are born.

Then, we are reconciled to everyone who has confessed Jesus as Lord, whether black, white, brown, red, or yellow. They are all our brothers and sisters. We have a new family, made of 90 million people in American and over 1.5 billion around the globe, who do not all look or sound alike. Our common ground is that they, like you, are covered by the blood of Jesus. Their burdens are mine and yours. We connect, not by race and nationalities, but by the blood of Jesus the Christ!

Imagine what our Christian colleges (now with only a two percent African American average enrollment and six to eight percent among people of color) and institutions, our housing, schools, banks, and places of worship might look like when led by "mighty warriors" like Gideon. Warriors who are following the charge of God to go in the strength they have been given, and to lead us to become the family that God has called us to be.

In their recent book, *The Church Enslaved: A Spirituality of Racial Reconciliation*, Tony Campolo and, African American theologian, Michael Battle, stated, "While overt racism has gone underground, subtle forms of racism exist that assume white superiority and the inferiority of people of color. Christianity has been deeply compromised by its participation in racism."

So, we need some among you who will "go in the strength that is yours," knowing that God is with you to break down every racial barrier, every wall of injustice and bigotry, and every vestige of unearned skin-color privilege. Then we can begin seeing one another by our blood ties to Jesus Christ, our Lord and Savior, and not according to our biological skin ties. Remember, *"There is no longer Jew or Greek, there is no longer slave or free, there is no longer male or female; for all of you are one in Christ Jesus"* (Galatians 3:28).

On the day of Pentecost, all the believers were gathered from different tribes and tongues and yet, *"they all heard the gospel in their own language."* 1 John 4:20 says, *"How can you say you love God who you have not seen, and hate your brother [or your sister] whom you see everyday."* It is not enough to simply say, "I don't hate anyone," and smugly stand by, while the divisions increase. The opposite of love is not hate; the opposite of love is indifference.

God is calling His people today to model the first century church described in the second chapter of the Book of Acts, verses 42-47: *"They devoted themselves to the apostles' teaching and to fellowship, to the breaking of bread and to prayer. Everyone was filled with awe and many wonders and miraculous signs were done by the apostles. All the believers were together and had everything in common. Selling their possessions and goods, they gave to anyone as they had need. Every day they continued to meet together in the temple courts. They broke bread in their homes and ate together with glad and sincere hearts, praising God and enjoying the favor of all the people. And the Lord added to their number daily those who were being saved."*

A second area where God is calling mighty warriors to go, in the strength that is theirs, and backed by the power of God, is the area of poverty and powerlessness for the poor. There are over 3,000 verses of scripture on God's concern for the poor. God is no respecter of persons, but He takes personally how we deal with institutional practices and structures that keep the poor in the position of poor.

Read a few of these scriptures and understand God's heart for the poor. Deuteronomy 15:4; Deuteronomy 15:11; Proverbs 14:31; Proverbs 19:17; Proverbs 21:13; Proverbs 22:16; Proverbs 29:14; Proverbs 29:4; Proverbs 31:9. Can you see in these passages that God is calling us to speak up for the people who have no voice, to fight for the rights of all those considered down-and-out, to speak out for justice, and to stand up for the poor and destitute?

Jesus began his earthly ministry by preaching *"The spirit of the Lord is upon me, for he has anointed me to preach good news to the poor. He has sent me to proclaim freedom for the prisoners and recovery of sight for the blind, to release the oppressed, to proclaim the year of the Lord's favor"* (Luke 4:18). Jesus ended his reading of the Book of Isaiah (Chapter 62) by saying, *"today this reading is accomplished in your hearing."* In other words, when I show up, these things happen. As God's ambassadors, mighty warriors for God, when we show up, good news is preached to the poor, the oppressed are set free, and those in prison are visited.

When mighty warriors show up, public policies that oppress the poor, will be advocated by those who politicians and public leaders will respond to. The reality is: poor children are more likely to drop out of school, end up in prison, end up as teen parents, and have a lower quality life. It takes only $10,000 - $15,000 a year to properly educate a child, but more than $60,000 a year to house them in prison.

It is not enough to send money! When the poor people of New Orleans were devastated by the killer hurricane, Katrina, they did not need only money. They needed the presence of loving and caring people, they needed to know that they were valued and would be treated, not as refugees, but as valued citizens in distress.

God did not send a check, he sent his only Son, Jesus Christ! Now, he wants to send you. Not as community service interns into poor neighborhoods, as a requirement for a "better" job, but God is calling you to go as a mighty warrior, in the strength that is yours, and backed by God's power. He is calling you to get angry with a righteous anger towards poverty, and, in the world's richest nation, to do something about it.

If you need some help getting started, I'll help you eliminate the excuses! Connect with the Christian Community Development Association to build partnerships with over 5,000 believers who are restoring at risk neighborhoods; join forces with Sojourners in Washington, DC and the Call to Renewal, who are treating the US Budget as a moral document and confronting members of congress about their decision to cut programs that sustain poor people while giving away millions to the wealthy; work with men like Dr. John Perkins and his Center for Racial Reconciliation in various cities; join women like Marian Wright Edelman in powerful lobbying for poor and disenfranchised youth of all backgrounds with the Children's Defense Fund; or work with Tony Campolo, who is raising up new generations of Gideon's army for both urban and global missions. Martin Luther King Jr.'s proclamation was right, "everyone can be great because everyone can serve."

Ask yourself a question: "What will it take for me to become a 'mighty warrior' who answers the call of God to go, in whatever strength God has given me, and deal with a myriad of issues that confront the world today?"

Allow me to suggest three things you should do: First understand who God is; secondly, know who you are; and thirdly, act with courage and go where God is calling you. Let's examine further. God is King of kings and Lord of lords. You are the King's kid. You are a member of the Kingdom of God, which is the live expression on earth of exactly what is going on in heaven. So, if nonbelievers want to know what heaven is like, all they have to do is to watch us! As they watch us, they should see how we love those who are different from us, how we worship with people of any denomination or background who are committed to worshipping Christ our King, how we resolve conflict, and how we have stopped worshipping our culture, skin color, backgrounds, and pedigrees, and have begun to live, and love those who love God.

We are Psalm's 8 people, created a little lower than God, crowned with glory and honor. Move beyond your personal doubts and insecurities, to make a commitment. Then, act, with courage, on the issues facing your generation. Dr. Billy Graham, whose extraordinary life and ministry spans eight decades, acted with courage, in spite of a hostile American media. Dr. Graham took a 1982 trip to Moscow, to preach the gospel in a mostly atheistic nation. When he returned, 10 years later, he returned to 50,000 people in a stadium built for 38,000, with another 30,000 watching the crusade on projection screens.

Dr. Maya Angelou said, "Courage is the most important human quality, because without it, you cannot consistently practice any other." Shakespeare said, "Cowards die many times before their deaths; The valiant never taste of death but once." One anonymous writer recorded, regarding Christianity:

"Christianity is not a voice in the wilderness, but a life in the world. It is not an idea in the air but feet on the ground, going God's way. It is not an exotic to be kept under glass, but a hardy plant to bear twelve months of fruits in all kinds of weather. Fidelity to duty is its root and branch. Nothing we can say to the Lord, no calling Him by great or dear names, can take the place of plain doing of His will. We may cry about the beauty of eating bread with Him in His kingdom, but it is wasted breath and a rootless hop, unless we plow and plant in His kingdom here and now. To remember Him at His table but forget Him at ours, is to have invested in bad securities. There is no substitute for plain, every-day goodness"

The same God who spoke to Gideon and his generation, is speaking to yours today. The same God who said "light be," and light was; who gave the snowflakes their assignments and the lightning bolts their destinations; who said, "with me nothing in impossible"; who said, "No weapon formed against you will prosper." He is God, who is the same yesterday, today, and forever.

That same God is calling you, "Mighty Warriors," and releasing you to "go in the strength that you have, in that name, which is above every name, the Name of Jesus Christ!" Your calling: Save your people; save our nation; save our world!

FOOTNOTES

[1] Rick Warren, The Purpose Driven Life (Grand Rapids, Michigan: Zondervan, 2002), 42.

[2] Ibid.

[3] Ibid.

[4] The United Methodist Hymnal (Nashville, Tennessee: Abingdon Press, 1992), 867.

[5] Warren, The Purpose Drive Life, 41.

[6] Brian K. Blount, True to Our Native Land: An African American New Testament Commentary (Minneapolis: Fortress Press, 2007),461.

[7] Ibid., 463.

[8] Ibid.

[9] Ibid.

[10] Ibid.

[11] Ibid.

[12] Ibid.

[13] Webster's New Collegiate Dictionary (Springfield, Massachusetts: G &C Merriam Company, 1981), 185.

[14] Gospellyrics.blogspot.com/2008/02/cast-your-burdens-unto-Jeus.html

[15] Michael P. Green, 1500 Illustrations for Biblical Preaching (Grand Rapids, Michigan: Baker Books, 2001), 363.

[16] Gen. 21-2

[17] Gen. 21-17

[18] Gen. 21-17

[19] Gen. 21-18

[20] Gen. 21-20

[21] Gen. 21:10

[22] Gen. 21:21

[23] Gen. 21:21

[24] King, Martin Luther, Dr. Strength to Love-Transformed Non-conformist, Fortress Press, Philadelphia, PA, 1981, pg 19.

About The Contributors

THE REV. DR. LESLIE D. CALLAHAN is a pastor, scholar, writer, and cultural critic. On May 17, 2009, she was called as the first female pastor of the historical 119-year old St. Paul's Baptist Church, located in the heart of Philadelphia. A gifted professor, Dr. Callahan, was a member of the faculty of the University of Pennsylvania as assistant professor of religious studies. She has also served as the Assistant Professor of Modern Church History and African American Studies at New York Theological Seminary. Her formal education includes the Bachelor of Arts in Religion from Harvard/Radcliffe and the Master of Divinity from Union Theological Seminary in the City of New York and the Doctor of Philosophy (PhD) degree in Religion from Princeton University. Noted for her preaching and teaching gifts, she was recognized in the June 2005 edition of the African American Pulpit as one of the "20 to Watch," outstanding African American ministers under age 40.

THE REV. DR. CLAUDETTE A. COPELAND serves as Co-founder and Pastor of New Creation Christian Fellowship in San Antonio, Texas. She received her undergraduate education at the University of Connecticut, in the field of Psychology. She earned her Master of Divinity in Pastoral Care and Counseling from the Interdenominational Theological Center in Atlanta, Georgia. She earned the Doctorate of Ministry Degree from United Theological Seminary in Dayton, Ohio. Licensed as an evangelist at age 18 (The Church of God in Christ) and ordained in 1979, she has served as a Hospital Chaplaincy, the Mission Field (in Haiti, South Africa, West Africa and East Africa). Reverend Copeland is the founder of Claudette Copeland Ministries, a national empowerment group for women. Dr. Copeland

211

made history as the first woman to offer the keynote address to the National MLK Jr. Commemorative March in a major urban venue, addressing over 80,000 persons in San Antonio for this great event (2004). Claudette is married to Bishop David M. Copeland.

THE REV. SHELETA FOMBY was licensed to preach in the year 2002. She received ordination as Itinerant Deacon in the African Methodist Episcopal (A.M.E.) Church in April 2007 and Itinerant Elder orders in April 2009. Rev. Fomby currently serves as the Minister to Women at Reid Temple AME Church, Inc. under the dynamic mantle of Rev. Dr. Lee P. Washington, Senior Pastor. A gifted preacher and teacher, Rev. Fomby has been privileged to proclaim the gospel on various national platforms. Most recently her sermons have been published in The African American Pulpit Journal. The same publication has recognized her as one of the "20 To Watch Under 40". Rev. Fomby holds a Bachelor of Science Degree from the University of MD (UMUC) and Masters of Divinity at Wesley Theological Seminary.

THE REV. DR. CECELIA E. GREENEBARR is an Itinerant Elder in the African Methodist Episcopal Church - presently serving in the Fourth District - Michigan Annual Conference as the pastor of Smith Chapel AME Church in Inkster, MI. Her pastoral experience includes over five years of service at Trinity AME Church in Detroit. She is the author of Guide My Feet: Ministry Transformed through Mentoring, a contributing author in This is My Story: Testimonies and Sermons of Black Women in Ministry, The African American Pulpit (Summer 2005), and When Pastors Pray: The Prayers and Psalms of Pastors. Rev. Dr. Greene Barr is a life member of Delta Sigma Theta Sorority, Inc. She is an honors graduate of North Carolina Agricultural and Technical State University with a Bachelor of Science degree in Industrial Technology in Manufacturing. Her theological education was completed at Princeton Theological Seminary where she earned a Master of Divinity degree and Ashland Theological Seminary where she earned a Doctor of Ministry degree in the area of Transformational Leadership. She is the wife of Theron Barr, Jr; they are the parents of Theron-Howard and Cecelia II.

BISHOP MILLICENT HUNTER is the Presiding Bishop of the Worship Center Worldwide Fellowship of Churches with 71 churches in the United States and South Africa. She is also Founder and Senior Pastor of The Baptist Worship Center of Philadelphia, Pennsylvania. Starting with five (5) members in a row house in West Philadelphia, this ministry has grown to over 4,000 members. Bishop Hunter is an award-winning author of several books. Her first book entitled Don't Die In The Winter...Your Season Is Coming was a bestseller. She was featured in Gospel Today Magazine as one of America's Top 10 Global Pacesetting Pastors, and in Charisma and Ebony magazine as a leading Pastor for World Evangelism. She is the founder of the National Association of Clergy Women, and the CEO of the Excell Community Development Corporation. She is the founder of The Excell Christian Academy. Dr. Hunter established The Worship Center Bible Training Institute in South Africa and the United States which trains and mentors students in Bible and Ministry. She has an extensive educational background having earned the degree of Doctor of Education.

THE REV. SHARMA D. LEWIS is a 1985 graduate of Mercer University, where she received a Bachelor of Science degree in Biology, and a 1988 graduate of West Georgia College, where she received a Master of Science degree in Biology. She served as a biologist in the academic and corporate sectors for several years. After answering God's call to ministry, she entered Gammon Seminary at the Interdenominational Theological Center (ITC) in Atlanta,

Georgia. While attending ITC she was inducted into Theta Phi Honor Society and was the recipient of numerous awards. In 1999, she earned a Master of Divinity in Biblical studies with honors. Rev. Lewis was ordained a Deacon in the UMC in 1999 and an Elder in 2002. Rev. Lewis traveled to Kericho, Kenya in 2007 with the Mission Society, to train clergy in the area of missions. Reverend Lewis is the Senior Pastor of Wesley Chapel UMC, McDonough, GA. She assumed this position on June 27, 2007, having served as Senior Pastor at Powers Ferry UMC, a cross-racial appointment, since 2004. Prior to her pastoral duties at Powers Ferry, she was an Associate Pastor at Ben Hill UMC from 1999-2004.

EVANGELIST SUSIE C. OWENS is a graduate of Bethel Bible Institute, where she earned an Associate of Arts degree in New Testament Studies in 1970. Understanding her call to teach, she pursued the field of education, graduating from Brooks College in 1972 with a Bachelor of Arts degree in Early Childhood Education. In May of 1999, she received a Master of Arts degree in Religious Studies from Howard University School of Divinity. She is the wife of Bishop Alfred A. Owens, Jr., D. Min., who is the pastor of Greater Mt. Calvary Holy Church in Washington, D.C. Evangelist Owens serves alongside her husband in ministry as the Co-Pastor of Greater Mt. Calvary Holy Church, a progressive, inner-city church with an adult membership of more than 7,000. She serves as Vice President and an Instructor of the Calvary Bible Institute, an accredited Bible School under Greater Mt. Calvary Holy Church. She is the author of two books Unless Two Agree and Memorable Moments. Finally, she is the proud mother of two children, Alfred Thomas and Kristel Moneek and grandmother of five Nathan, Darian, Nicholas, William, and Kaiden.

THE REV. DR. VANNETTA R. RATHER earned a Bachelor of Science Degree (Magna Cum Laude) in Human Services from Springfield College in Springfield, Massachusetts. In 2004, Rev. Rather earned a Master of Divinity from the Wesley Theological Seminary in Washington, DC. In 2009 Rev. Rather earned a Doctor of Ministry with a concentration in preaching from the Wesley Theological Seminary. Rev. Rather serves as Associate Pastor of Youth and College Ministries at the Mt. Ennon Baptist Church in Clinton, MD under the leadership of Dr. Delman Coates, Sr. Pastor. She was honored by the National Coalition of One Hundred Black Women, Inc., Northern Virginia Chapter to receive the Ebony Image Award for her work with youth in 2009. Rev. Rather's passions include preaching, teaching and the worshipping arts. She has taught liturgical dance for over ten years and has been fortunate and blessed to have ministered with gospel artists such as Kirk Franklin, Yolanda Adams and Byron Cage. The worshipping arts ministry provided Rev. Rather with opportunities to minister at both the Warner and Lincoln Theaters in Washington, DC and in Bermuda.

THE REV. DR TRENACE NICOLE RICHARDSON acknowledged the call to preach the gospel while in college and was licensed to preach in April 1999 at Shalom Ministries Christian Center where Rev. Florida Morehead is the pastor. Trenace is the Director of Operations at Zion Church in Largo, Maryland where Rev. Keith Battle is the pastor. Trenace is the founder of Young Women in Ministry, Inc., which is a non-profit organization that provides women in ministry an opportunity to come together in support of each other as they face similar challenges in ministry. Trenace attended Elizabeth City State University where she earned a Bachelor of Arts degree in English/Secondary Education, Magna Cum Laude (with high honors). She taught English at Bowie High School, while at the same time attending Howard University where she obtained a Master of Divinity. She graduated with a 3.9 GPA and received the Timms Outstanding Religious Educator Award. In May 2009, Trenace earned a doctoral degree in Higher Education Administration at The George Washington University.

EVANGELIST SANDRA RILEY is well sought conference speaker, seminar presenter, and women and youth workshop presenter who has obtained national and international acclaim across denominational lines. As President and CEO of "Just for U Ministries," Sandra Riley operates in the highest level of excellence in ministry. She was ordained at the Bethel Pentecostal Church Abundant Life Center, in Grand Rapids, Michigan under the Pastorate of the late Bishop William C. Abney. She is presently an associate minister at Lighthouse Full Center Church, under the Pastorate of her cousin, Dr. Marvin L. Sapp. As an accomplished businesswoman Sandra is also President and CEO of Rabah Group LLC, Inc., a real estate investment company specializing in rentals to low-income families. Sandra Riley is featured in First Family Film's documentary of women in ministry entitled "Every Soldier Counts" and the African American Pulpit Journal recently named Sandra one of the "Emerging Voices" who will shape the future of the African American Church.

THE REV. DR. ELIZABETH REGINA SAPP JONES accepted her call to preach the gospel in 1995 while attending Ebenezer AME Church in Ft. Washington, MD. She currently serves as Minister to Women at Messiah Baptist Church, in Bridgeport, CT where her husband, Rev. Tyrone P. Jones IV serves as pastor. Together, they have two beautiful children, Tyrone Phillip and Emani Regina.Dr. Jones holds a Master of Divinity degree from Howard University School of Divinity. In 2008, Dr. Jones obtained an Executive Master of Business Administration degree from the University of Connecticut and a Doctor of Ministry (DMin) degree in Pastoral Counseling from Hebrew Union College in New York. Dr. Jones is a proud member of Delta Sigma Theta Sorority, Inc. and is the founder and Executive Director of Nephesh Ministries, a ministry dedicated to "Breathing the Breath of Christ into Every Living Soul."

THE REV. DR. JASMINE "JAZZ' SCULARK—affectionately known as "Dr. Jazz," is a native of Trinidad and Tobago. She was ordained in 1999 at the Mt. Olivet Baptist church, where Dr. Charles E. Booth is the Senior Pastor. She currently serves as the Senior pastor of Shiloh Baptist church of York, PA. She is the Founder of Daughters of Thunder Ministries, Inc., a ministry that assists the local church in providing holistic, life changing ministries to youth, singles, young adults and women. Dr. Jazz is a graduate of the Practical Bible College in Vestal, NY and Washington Bible College in Lanham, MD. She received her Masters of Divinity Degree from Trinity Lutheran Seminary in Columbus, OH. In December 2007 she received her D.Min Degree from the United Theological Seminary, in Dayton, OH. Dr. Jazz formed the Empowerment Community Development Corporation in 2003- a ministry designed to provide computer training classes for seniors and teens in partnership with the Capital City Project and After School Tutoring Program and Summer Program—"Smart Kids for Christ." Well sought preacher, she has preached at the Howard University's School of Divinity, Shaw University and the Hampton Minister's Conference.

THE REV. DR. GINA MARCIA STEWART has led the congregation of Christ Missionary Baptist Church for 13 years. On March 4, 1995, she was elected by majority vote to serve as the pastor of Christ Missionary Baptist Church. She is the first African American female elected to serve an established African American Baptist congregation in Memphis and Shelby County. More than 3,000 persons have united with CMBC under her leadership since 1995. Dr. Stewart is currently serving as a Team Leader for the Pastoral Excellence Program for Lott Carey International, a development and advocacy organization. In addition to serving as a Team Leader, she currently serves as a Co-Convener for the Women in Ministry Conference-Dr. Cynthia L. Hale, Convener and a Trustee for the Samuel DeWitt Proctor Pastors Conference. She also serves as a board member for the National Civil Rights Museum, Bread for the World and is a member of the Advisory Board for The African American Pulpit.

THE REV. DR. BARBARA WILLIAMS-SKINNER is president of Skinner Leadership Institute (SLI). Skinner Leadership Institute exists to produce a new generation of leaders who are technically excellent and spiritually mature. She is a nationally recognized spiritual leader, teacher, lecturer and writer, having earned her undergraduate degree from San Francisco State University, a Master of Social Work degree and a law degree from the University of California at Los Angeles. Dr. Williams-Skinner has also earned Master of Divinity and Doctorate of Ministry degrees at Howard University School of Divinity. She is the author of numerous articles including "The Power of Love," "Been There, Done That: Why African American Christians Resist Racial Reconciliation," "Why and How Would Jesus Vote," and "Obama, the Black Church, and the Promise of Reconciliation." Dr. Williams-Skinner is included in 2008 Presidential Who's Who Among Business and Professional Achievers.

ABOUT THE CO-EDITOR
REV. DR. CYNTHIA L. HALE

THE REV. DR. CYNTHIA L. HALE is the founding and Senior Pastor of the Ray of Hope Christian Church in Decatur, Georgia. Ray of Hope has an active membership of 5,000 and an average of 1,500 in worship each Sunday morning. Ray of Hope has been honored by the 700 Club as Church of the Week and was also recognized in the book, Excellent Protestant Congregations: The Guide to Best Places and Practice, as one of 300 excellent Protestant congregations in the United States.

Dr. Hale is a native of Roanoke, Virginia. Her natural talent in music led her to study at Hollins University in Virginia, from which she received her Bachelor of Arts degree. She holds a Master of Divinity degree from Duke University and a Doctor of Ministry degree from United Theological Seminary, Dayton, Ohio. Dr. Hale holds five Honorary Doctor of Divinity degrees, with the most recent conferred by the Interdenominational Theological Center, Atlanta, Georgia.

As a woman of vision, Dr. Hale is revered locally, nationally and internationally for her leadership, integrity, and compassion. Dr. Hale serves on an array of boards. In September 2005, she convened her first Women In Ministry Conference that hosted women from various stages in ministry. Dr. Hale was inducted into the African American Biographies Hall of Fame and the Martin Luther King's Board of

Preachers of Morehouse College. Selected by Senator Barack Obama and the Democratic Party, she gave the opening invocation at the 2008 Democratic National Convention. In 2009, she was privileged to participate at the National Prayer Service for the inauguration of President Barack Obama. Later in 2009, Dr. Hale was appointed to serve on the President's Commission on White House Fellowships. She also served as Co-Chair for "Women In Ministry for Obama." Additionally, Dr. Hale was featured on CNN's documentary "Black in America Part 2."

Dr. Hale has received numerous honors and recognitions. She received the Outstanding Religious Leader Award presented by Nu Lambda Omega Chapter of Alpha Kappa Alpha Sorority, Inc. In 2008, her sermon entitled "It's Time for the Silent Giant to Speak Up" was published in The African American Pulpit Journal. She is also a contributor to the book, "Power in the Pulpit II: How America's Most Effective Black Preachers Prepare Their Sermons." Also in 2008, Dr. Hale received the Trombone Award presented by the Rainbow Push Coalition, and she received the Religious Excellence Award presented by Alpha Phi Alpha Fraternity, Inc.

Dr. Hale has been in ministry for 30 years. Her ministerial gift has drawn thousands, young and old, to witness the anointing on a woman totally sold out for the Kingdom of God. She has traveled abroad preaching the Gospel of Jesus Christ, sharing the "Good News" in Africa, Australia, Europe, the Caribbean, and South America. Dr. Hale is a woman on a mission to impact and transform this present world into the Kingdom of God.

ABOUT THE EDITOR
REV. DARRYL D. SIMS

Darryl D. Sims earned his Bachelor of Science degree in Hotel and Restaurant Management from Chicago State University in 1990. He was licensed to preach the gospel at Metropolitan Baptist Church in January of 1997, and served as a Sunday School Teacher for youth ages 15 to 18, from 1996-1998. In 1999, he graduated with a Masters in Divinity from the Howard University School of Divinity.

At Howard, he served as the graduate assistant to the Dean, Clarence G. Newsome. In May of 1999, Darryl became the Minister of Men and Evangelism at Mt. Olivet Baptist Church (Columbus, Ohio), and was the coordinator of the Church's After-school program, designed for improving the spiritual and educational development of urban elementary male students. Darryl also created and chaired the first Men's Conference and developed outreach initiatives to bring the Church and the community together.

Darryl Sims is the founder and president of Evangucation Ministries, Inc., which combines "evangelism" and "education" to improve the spiritual formation and educational development of African Americans.

Darryl is the editor, of three books entitled, *Sound the Trumpet: Messages to Empower African American Males*, published by Judson Press in January of 2003, and *Sound the Trumpet, Again: Messages to Empower African American Males* published by Judson in January of 2005, and *Evangelizing and Empowering the Black Male*, published by MMGI

Books in June of 2009. He currently serves as an Associate Pastor of Third Baptist Church in Chicago, IL, under the leadership of the Senior Pastor Dr. Alan V. Ragland. Darryl Sims is also the Managing Partner of MMGI Books, an African American Christian publishing company that specializes in thematic Christian products that seeks to address the social challenges within our society. The company produces material that is Christ-centered and ecumenical in its content.

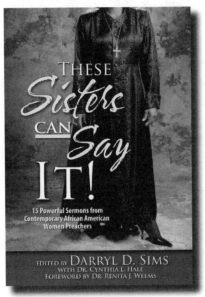

Journal For My Journey

_____

_____

_____

_____

_____

_____

_____

_____

_____

_____

_____

_____

_____

_____

_____

_____

_____

Journal For My Journey

_____

_____

_____

_____

_____

_____

_____

_____

_____

_____

_____

_____

_____

_____

_____

_____

_____

_____

_____

Journal For My Journey

_____

_____

_____

_____

_____

_____

_____

_____

_____

_____

_____

_____

_____

_____

_____

_____

_____

_____

Journal For My Journey

_____

_____

_____

_____

_____

_____

_____

_____

_____

_____

_____

_____

_____

_____

_____

_____

_____

_____

_____

_____

Journal For My Journey

_____

_____

_____

_____

_____

_____

_____

_____

_____

_____

_____

_____

_____

_____

_____

_____

_____

_____

Journal For My Journey

_____

_____

_____

_____

_____

_____

_____

_____

_____

_____

_____

_____

_____

_____

_____

_____

_____

_____

Journal For My Journey

_____

_____

_____

_____

_____

_____

_____

_____

_____

_____

_____

_____

_____

_____

_____

_____

_____

Journal For My Journey

_____

_____

_____

_____

_____

_____

_____

_____

_____

_____

_____

_____

_____

_____

_____

_____

_____

_____

_____

_____

_____

Journal For My Journey

_____

_____

_____

_____

_____

_____

_____

_____

_____

_____

_____

_____

_____

_____

_____

_____

_____

_____

Journal For My Journey

Journal For My Journey

Journal For My Journey

_____

_____

_____

_____

_____

_____

_____

_____

_____

_____

_____

_____

_____

_____

_____

_____

_____

_____

_____

_____

_____

Journal For My Journey

Journal For My Journey

_____

_____

_____

_____

_____

_____

_____

_____

_____

_____

_____

_____

_____

_____

_____

_____

_____

_____

_____

_____

_____

Journal For My Journey

_____

_____

_____

_____

_____

_____

_____

_____

_____

_____

_____

_____

_____

_____

_____

_____

_____

_____

Journal For My Journey

_____

_____

_____

_____

_____

_____

_____

_____

_____

_____

_____

_____

_____

_____

_____

_____

_____

_____

_____

_____

Journal For My Journey

_____

_____

_____

_____

_____

_____

_____

_____

_____

_____

_____

_____

_____

_____

_____

_____

_____

_____

_____

Journal For My Journey

_____

_____

_____

_____

_____

_____

_____

_____

_____

_____

_____

_____

_____

_____

_____

_____

_____

_____

_____

Journal For My Journey

_____

_____

_____

_____

_____

_____

_____

_____

_____

_____

_____

_____

_____

_____

_____

_____

_____